GOOD ⋆ OLD ⋆ DAYS®

Live It Again™
1959

Dear Friends,

As 1959 emerged, we continued to do what had been done for generations. We lived, we loved, we celebrated, and we anticipated what might be just around the corner. We delighted in all that was fresh and new as we enjoyed the journey that is life.

What was new for 1959? Alaska and Hawaii were the latest states to join the Union, sparking celebrations and a new flag design as the 48 states expanded to become 50. New television shows captured our attention. *Bonanza* corralled TV audiences in the way of Westerns, going on to entertain viewers for 14 seasons. Other new shows included the police drama *The Untouchables* and the situation comedy *The Many Loves of Dobie Gillis*.

> *We delighted in all that was fresh and new as we enjoyed the journey that is life.*

More new developments were in the works. We were on the brink of a new era in space as the names of the first astronauts for Project Mercury were revealed. These seven men, including John Glenn, Scott Carpenter and Alan Shepard, became national heroes and household names. The latest sensation in the world of toys, the fashion doll named Barbie®, was born. She was designed and named by Ruth Handler, one of the founders of Mattel. Barbie was an immediate success and grew into a toy empire that included doll clothes and an amazing array of accessories.

All of the years of the fabulous fifties were filled with the newness of increasing prosperity, the baby and housing boom, the growth of television and more choices in stores than we could have ever imagined. As the last year of the decade dawned, we were flooded with sentiments about the past, present and future. With a sense of nostalgia, we prepared to wave goodbye to a wonderful era. Reveling in the present, we lived 1959 with gusto. We also dreamily considered the future, anticipating the new experiences that would await us. Would our dreams come true?

Contents

NASA/COURTESY OF NASA IMAGES.

© GETTY IMAGES

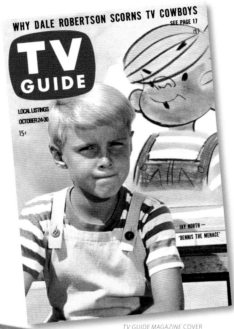

TV GUIDE MAGAZINE COVER COURTESY OF TV GUIDE MAGAZINE, LLC © 1959

AMERICAN OPTICAL CO.

© 1959 SEPS

REPRINTED WITH PERMISSION FROM FORD MOTOR CO.

1959 Quiz

1. What were the names of the two monkeys that NASA sent into space in May 1959?

2. Who starred in the TV show *Wanted: Dead or Alive*?

3. What was the top-selling book in 1959?

4. Who played the beatnik role of Maynard G. Krebs on the TV show *The Many Loves of Dobie Gillis*?

5. What famous fashion doll debuted in 1959?

6. What was the original name for Cheerios cereal?

7. What was the No. 1 movie in 1959?

8. Who sang the top hit song "Mack the Knife?"

Answers are found in this book and on page 127

One of the stars
of *The Shaggy
Dog* was Annette
Funicello,
known for her
television role as a
Mouseketeer. This
was her debut
movie role.

Tops *at the* Box Office

Ben-Hur

The Shaggy Dog

Some Like It Hot

Operation Petticoat

Pillow Talk

Imitation of Life

North by Northwest

The Nun's Story

Solomon and Sheba

On the Beach

At the Cinema

Among the outstanding movies of 1959 was the epic *Ben-Hur*, winning 11 Academy Awards, including an Oscar for Best Picture and Best Actor for Charlton Heston. The film was shot in Rome and was about a Jewish prince who was sent into slavery, regained his freedom and then returned for revenge. *Some Like It Hot* was a comedy about two musicians who witness a mob hit and flee the state disguised as women in an all-girl band. Life gets complicated as they attempt to keep their true identities hidden.

   The Shaggy Dog was another top movie, and the first-ever Walt Disney live-action comedy.

Charlton Heston starred as Judah Ben-Hur in the No. 1 movie of the year, set at the beginning of the first century. Heston had about a month to learn how to drive a chariot properly for *Ben-Hur*. The outdoor sets constructed for the chariot race were the largest built at the time. The film used over 1 million props and was shot over a period of nine months at Rome's Cinecittà Studios.

Tony Curtis and Jack Lemmon certainly enjoyed the ladies while on the run from the mob and disguised as women. Marilyn Monroe won a Golden Globe for her role in *Some Like It Hot*.

At the Cinema

© GETTY IMAGES

The popular acting team Doris Day and Rock Hudson star in the comedy *Pillow Talk*. It was the first of several movies they did together. In the movie, they share a telephone line and dislike each other until a romantic spark is lit. The movie won an Oscar for Best Writing, Story and Screenplay.

THE WEATHER
City and Surroundings.
Snow. Colder
Rain: a few showers

The Metro Daily News

FINAL EDITION

VOLUME 67 — No. 144

THE ASSOCIATED PRESS

20 PAGES

FIVE CENTS

JANUARY 3, 1959

ALASKA BECOMES THE 49TH STATE IN THE UNION

Cary Grant and James Mason look up from their table at Eva Marie Saint in this dining room scene from Alfred Hitchcock's film *North by Northwest*. The thriller was about a 2,000 mile chase that blazed a trail of terror to a mesmerizing, spine-chilling finish atop Mount Rushmore.

Simone Signoret and Charlton Heston hold their Oscars at the Academy Awards Ceremony. Heston won Best Actor for his performance in *Ben-Hur*. Signoret won Best Actress for her breakthrough role in *A Room at the Top*.

GETTY IMAGES

Movie Trivia

Q. What 1959 movie starred Sandra Dee and Troy Donahue as a young couple in love?

A. *A Summer Place*

© GETTY IMAGES

Sandra Dee and Lana Turner star in *Imitation of Life*. The movie revolves around the challenges of raising rebellious daughters and a mother who single-mindedly pursues stardom at the expense of home life.

© GETTY IMAGES

At left, Lydia and Rossano Brazzi attend a Hollywood party with Mitzi Gaynor and her husband, Jack Bean. Rossano and Mitzi starred in the movie *South Pacific*. Mary Martin, upper right with her husband Richard Halliday, was often remembered for her Broadway role as Peter in *Peter Pan*.

Mary Ann Mobley, representing Mississippi, was crowned Miss America 1959. She was later successful in film, television, Broadway and as a documentary filmmaker. In 1967, she married Gary Collins, actor and talk-show host.

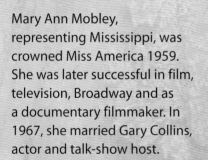

Robert F. Kennedy, politician and member of the famous Kennedy family, is shown with wife Ethel and their children. Mrs. Kennedy was expecting their seventh of eleven children when this photo was taken in 1959.

Famous Celebrities

We are fascinated with celebrities because they represent a lifestyle we wish we had. They are paid large sums of money for their talents, and the money they make allows them to do things most of us can only dream about. The paparazzi follow their every move, providing us with interesting glimpses of their private lives.

Jack Webb was television's top cop for his role as Joe Friday on *Dragnet*. He is pictured with his wife, Jackie Loughery, who won the Miss USA beauty pageant in 1952.

FAMOUS BIRTHDAYS

Linda Blair, January 22 actress
(Regan of *The Exorcist*)
Sade Adu, January 16 singer
"Smooth Operator"

Tony Curtis grew up in the tenements of Manhattan and became a successful heartthrob in the 1950s. In 1951, he married Janet Leigh, an accomplished actress. The couple had two daughters, Kelly and Jamie Lee, shown at right. Jamie Lee also became a famous actress.

Famous Celebrities

Oscar Robertson was a University of Cincinnati basketball star who went on to become a big name in professional basketball. "I like to win at anything I play, whether it's basketball or table tennis," he said.

Below is Southern Methodist University coach Bill Meek and quarterback Don Meredith, who later played for the Dallas Cowboys. Meredith also became an actor and sports commentator.

Sen. Hubert Humphrey of Minnesota, above, interacts with Sen. Lyndon B. Johnson of Texas. Johnson became the U.S. President and Humphrey his vice-president following the death of President John F. Kennedy in 1963.

Nelson Rockefeller, New York's governor in 1959, was appointed vice president by President Gerald Ford in 1974 after President Richard M. Nixon's resignation.

© 1959 SEPS

Frank Sinatra and Bing Crosby, both well-known singers and actors, are rehearsing for a TV special, *The Bing Crosby Show*.

Actor and singer Dean Martin, right, began his show business career at age 17 by singing in nightclubs near his hometown of Steubenville, Ohio. He was best known for his partnership in comedy with Jerry Lewis.

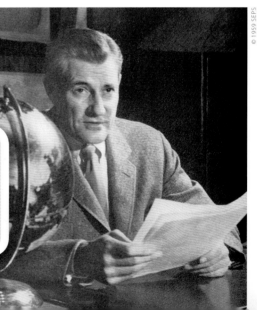

© 1959 SEPS

CBS news journalist Eric Sevareid enjoyed an extensive and distinguished career, becoming a commentator on the *CBS Evening News* for which he received Emmy and Peabody awards.

MEMORABLE QUOTE

"A man who can't smell the mood of the Senate has no business being leader."

—Sen. Lyndon B. Johnson

Top Hits of 1959

"Mack the Knife"
Bobby Darin

"The Battle of New Orleans"
Johnny Horton

"Venus"
Frankie Avalon

"Stagger Lee"
Lloyd Price

"The Three Bells"
The Browns

"Lonely Boy"
Paul Anka

"Come Softly to Me"
The Fleetwoods

"Smoke Gets In Your Eyes"
The Platters

"Heartaches by the Number"
Guy Mitchell

"Sleep Walk"
Santo & Johnny

Music Entertained Us

What happened to rock 'n' roll? A glance at the top hits of 1959 reveals the absence of the style due mostly to Elvis Presley's Army service and the death of Buddy Holly in a plane crash. In their places, artists like Bobby Darin, Frankie Avalon and Paul Anka produced the top hits. A combination of pop and light rock 'n' roll ruled the charts for the year.

Teen idol Frankie Avalon performs on *American Bandstand*. His song "Venus" was a big hit. Six more of his easy-listening records also made it into the Top 40 in 1959, including *"I'll Wait for You"* and *"A Boy Without a Girl."*

© GETTY IMAGES

In 1958, Bobby Darin wrote and recorded "Splish Splash," which became his first hit. In 1959, he hit the big time with "Mack the Knife," winning two Grammy awards.

© GETTY IMAGES

Paul Anka launched his career at age 16 with his first hit song, "Diana." By 1959, he traveled the world to perform dreamy love songs like "Lonely Boy" for enthusiastic audiences.

© GETTY IMAGES

© GETTY IMAGES

Herb Reed, David Lynch, Tony Williams, Zola Taylor and Paul Robi united as the popular singing group, The Platters. They became successful by updating older standard songs. "Smoke Gets In Your Eyes" was their well-remembered 1959 hit.

Dick Clark, left, was the host of *American Bandstand*, a regular feature on ABC. Clark spun the latest records while his guests danced. Above, three couples chosen by Clark from the studio audience demonstrate their dance techniques.

Back in the 1950s, many record stores had listening booths. Customers like those at right could listen to songs before deciding what records to buy.

Music Entertained Us

The television show *American Bandstand* kept viewers updated on the latest music and dance steps. Emcee Dick Clark's good looks and appealing smile had become synonymous with popular music. Teenagers all over America rushed home from school each day to watch the program.

Tragedy struck the music industry on February 3, 1959, a date often referred to as "The Day the Music Died." A plane crash took the life of rising rock 'n' roll star Buddy Holly. A lean Texan from Lubbock, Holly wrote most of his songs himself, adding a new range to the musical style.

Buddy Holly was interested in country music before he saw a live Elvis Presley show in 1955. At that point, he concentrated on rock 'n' roll. Though his life ended early, his music never really died as his work was released and covered by other bands throughout the 1960s.

© GETTY IMAGES

The Metro Daily News

THE WEATHER
City at Rate—Rec.
Snow, Colder
Stalin in Here Affairs

VOLUME 67 — No. 35

FINAL EDITION

10 PAGES   FIVE CENTS

FEBRUARY 3, 1959

PLANE CRASH KILLS THREE MUSICIANS

Rock legend Buddy Holly is found dead near Clear Lake, Iowa, along with fellow rockers Ritchie Valens and J.P. "Big Bopper" Richardson.

The Electronic Review

In order to be able to use the words "new and improved" in advertisements, electronics manufacturers employed scientists and inventors to discover ways to enhance their products. Stereophonic sound, push-button alarm-clock controls and more-automated camera features were among the selling points of the electronics of 1959. Music became more portable with small record players, like those shown at left that sold for $79.90 to $139.90.

← Now enjoy the magic of Magnavox wherever you go

NEW FROM KODAK!

$137.50

$34.50

$124.50

$84.50

$124.50

$74.50

Kodak welcomes you to the **Automatic Age** in photography

NEW GENERAL ELECTRIC
PUSH-BUTTON CLOCK RADIO with SNOOZ-ALARM®

REPRINTED WITH PERMISSION FROM GENERAL ELECTRIC CO.

Magnavox quality came to stereo portables with all the exciting concert tone and dimensional realism of stereophonic music.

1959 ARGUS INC.

1959 ARGUS INC.

COURTESY OF ZENITH ELECTRONICS LLC

The Argus camera above came with a light meter, case, flash and lifetime guarantee for $64.95. The 35mm camera at left, complete with meter, case and flash, sold for $139.95.

argus®
DIVISION OF SYLVANIA ELECTRIC PRODUCTS INC.

The Zenith Crescendo stereo above captured the full depth and range of sound. This unit had an AM/FM radio along with the phonograph and was priced at $700.

TAKE THIS TEST ON TV MANNERS   SEE PAGE 5

TV GUIDE

Local Listings · Feb. 28 - March 6

15¢

RICHARD BOONE

TELEVISION—A WOMAN'S GAME?

TV GUIDE

Local Listings · May 30—June 5

15¢

STEVE McQUEEN OF 'WANTED—DEAD OR ALIVE'

A scene of *Gunsmoke* is filmed on a soundstage at California Studios. The show ran for 20 seasons from 1955 to 1975, making it one of the most enduring prime-time, live-action dramas.

Have Gun—Will Travel starred the dapper Richard Boone, above. *Wanted: Dead or Alive* launched Steve McQueen's transition from TV to the big screen.

Perry Mason starred Raymond Burr, left, the defense attorney who managed to piece together mystery puzzles in the nick of time.

TV Land

Tops on the tube

The familiar Westerns and detective thrillers continued to monopolize TV programming. *Gunsmoke* was the top-rated show for the year, a position the show had occupied since 1957. *Perry Mason* was TV's most successful lawyer series, based on novelist Erle Stanley Gardner's books. Actor Steve McQueen starred in *Wanted: Dead or Alive*. He portrayed an Old West bounty hunter during the last half of the 19th century.

Television networks were shaken by quiz show scandals in 1959. Evidence proved that many contestants had been given advance knowledge of questions or answers. As a result, most of the once-popular giveaway programs were cancelled.

GETTY IMAGES

Tops on Television

Gunsmoke
CBS

Wagon Train
NBC

Have Gun—Will Travel
CBS

The Danny Thomas Show
CBS

The Red Skelton Show
CBS

Father Knows Best
CBS

77 Sunset Strip
ABC

The Price Is Right
NBC

Wanted: Dead or Alive
CBS

Perry Mason
CBS

In a scene from *77 Sunset Strip*, the glamorous private-detective team Efrem Zimbalist Jr., far left, and Roger Smith, second from the left, worked out of a Hollywood office. They played characters Stu Bailey and Jeff Spencer, former government officers. In the center is Edd Byrnes as "Kookie," and at the far right is Louis Quinn as Roscoe.

TV Land

1959's new shows

From left to right are actors Jerry Paris, Abel Fernandez, Robert Stack and Nicholas Georgiade from *The Untouchables*. A police drama set in Chicago during the 1930s, the show brought big ratings to ABC.

The Many Loves of Dobie Gillis centered on the life of Dobie Gillis, a teenage boy who longed for popularity and beautiful girlfriends. The cast included Dwayne Hickman as Dobie Gillis, Sheila James, who played Zelda Gilroy, and Bob Denver as beatnik Maynard G. Krebs, who later became famous for his role on *Gilligan's Island*.

WHAT TEEN-AGE BOYS LOOK FOR IN GIRLS
see page 20

TV GUIDE

LOCAL LISTINGS · DECEMBER 5-11

15¢

GAYLE POLAYES, JOAN CHANDLER AND DWAYNE HICKMAN OF 'DOBIE GILLIS'

"This is their last chance. If they get the giggles this time, they're through."

The cast of *Bonanza* are shown above. Left to right are Michael Landon as Little Joe, Dan Blocker as Hoss, Pernell Roberts as Adam, and Lorne Green as Ben Cartwright. The show featured the Cartwright family who lived on a large ranch called the Ponderosa.

Television Shows Debuting in 1959

The Bell Telephone Hour

Bonanza

Bourbon Street Beat

Hawaiian Eye

The Many Loves of Dobie Gillis

Markham

Men Into Space

Rawhide

The Rebel

The Twilight Zone

The Untouchables

Clint Eastwood, center, was one of the stars of *Rawhide*. The show revolved around the organizers and runners of communal cattle drives and the people they met during their travels. The trail boss was Gil Favor, played by Eric Fleming, and his right-hand man was Rowdy Yates, played by Eastwood. The show's theme song was sung by Frankie Laine.

TV Land

Kids' favorites

Indulge in a glimpse of the popular shows we watched as kids. The fun cartoon, *The Bullwinkle Show*, debuted in 1959. The program featured the ongoing adventures of Bullwinkle, a dim-witted but lovable moose from Frostbite Falls, Minn., and his small pal, Rocky, a flying squirrel who wore an aviator's cap. The *Dennis the Menace* comic strip by Hank Ketchum was brought to life and televised for the first time in 1959. Dennis, played by Jay North, was a young boy who tried to be helpful, but somehow usually managed to make matters worse! *Lassie*, the classic and long-running children's adventure series, featured a collie. In 1959, her owner in the series was Timmy Martin, played by Jon Provost.

The Tales of Wells Fargo was so popular with children that Western toys were sold featuring the show's name.

1959 MONTGOMERY WARD

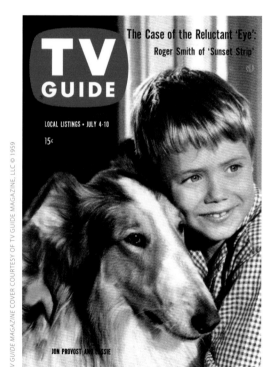

TV GUIDE MAGAZINE COVER COURTESY OF TV GUIDE MAGAZINE, LLC © 1959

The Case of the Reluctant 'Eye': Roger Smith of 'Sunset Strip'

TV GUIDE

LOCAL LISTINGS • JULY 4-10

15¢

JON PROVOST AND LASSIE

THE WEATHER

The Metro Daily News
FINAL EDITION

MARCH 9, 1959

BARBIE® DEBUTS
Mattel's Barbie doll is introduced at the American Toy Fair.

© GETTY IMAGES

The long-suffering parents on *Dennis the Menace* put up with their son as much as possible, which was more than could be said of next-door neighbor, Mr. Wilson.

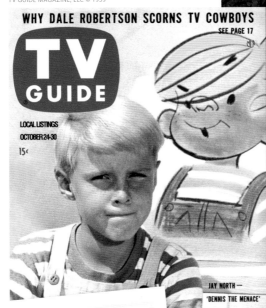

WHY DALE ROBERTSON SCORNS TV COWBOYS
SEE PAGE 17

TV GUIDE

LOCAL LISTINGS
OCTOBER 24-30
15¢

JAY NORTH —
'DENNIS THE MENACE'

Television for Youngsters

The Bullwinkle Show

Dennis the Menace

Fury

The Heckle and Jeckle Cartoon Show

Howdy Doody

Lassie

Leave It to Beaver

The Mickey Mouse Club

The Mighty Mouse Playhouse

Paul Winchell and Jerry Mahoney

Ruff and Reddy

The Tales of Wells Fargo

Bobby Diamond starred as young Joey Newton and Peter Graves as Jim Newton in *Fury*. In the photo, the horse Fury is dressed as Santa, complete with white beard. The popular adventure show related the friendships and conflicts of a bachelor, his adopted son and their horse. Good always triumphed over evil for these fictional characters!

FIRST TRANSISTOR, BATTERY-POWERED PORTABLE TV!

New PHILCO *Safari* plays anywhere without plugging in...even in bright sunlight!

PHILCO
QUALITY FIRST!

This tiny model was the first portable TV to be battery-powered. The battery was rechargeable with a built-in recharger. The cost was $250, and the rechargeable battery was $5.25 extra.

1960 Admiral Wide Angle 23″ TV
New Stereophonic Phono
New FM·AM Radio
All in one decorator cabinet

Above, The Sovereign, Model STR24M97

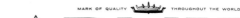

MARK OF QUALITY ☰ THROUGHOUT THE WORLD
ADMIRAL

Admirals Sold in 90 countries... Manufactured in the U.S.A., Argentina, Australia, Brazil, Canada, Italy, Mexico, Philippines, and Uruguay. Admiral Corp., Chicago 47, Ill., and Port Credit, Canada.

This Admiral television had squared corners like a movie screen. Viewers could see 20 square inches more than an ordinary 21-inch TV. The pull-out stereo phonograph and AM/FM radio made this model a complete entertainment center.

ADMIRAL ANNOUNCES THE WORLD'S FIRST PORTABLE TV with WIRELESS REMOTE CONTROL!

Admiral SON-R wireless remote control, world's smallest and finest, tunes this new ☼ space age portable...the most versatile TV ever created! Take it to any room. Tune from anywhere in the room... from the comfort of your bed or easy chair. Wireless SON-R turns your new Admiral portable TV on-off, changes channels, adjusts volume to 4 levels! SON-R TV from $199⁹⁵.*

MARK OF QUALITY THROUGHOUT THE WORLD
Admiral

Sold in 90 countries...manufactured in the U.S.A., Argentina, Australia, Brazil, Canada, Italy, Mexico, Philippines, and Uruguay • Admiral Corp., Chicago 47, Ill., and Port Credit, Canada

Television Options

Television, the most innovative electronic item of the 1950s, steadily drew more viewers. In 1959, about 42 million homes had televisions, with some families already owning two sets. Advertisers emphasized the beautiful finishes of some cabinets that made them look like fine pieces of furniture. These units came with a high price tag. The Zenith model at right sold for $525.

GENERAL ⓖⓔ **ELECTRIC**

Only Zenith combines the beauty of fine furniture with the convenience of Space Command® remote TV tuning

The quality goes in before the name goes on

FAMOUS BIRTHDAYS
Tom Arnold, March 6 actor, comic
Fabio Lanzoni, March 15 model, actor

General Electric televisions stayed on the cutting edge of technology with electrostatic tweeters, four-way wireless remote controls and modern styling.

Our Favorite Treats

A sugary reward can entice even the pickiest of eaters to finish that last spoonful of peas or tuna casserole. Many of us grew up hearing our parents say, "Clean your plate so you can have dessert!" Sweet treats were often used as rewards for good behavior. Cookies, candy and gum not only tasted heavenly, but also made us feel special.

CHOCOLATE TURKISH
Crack it Up!
VANILLA TURKISH
Crack it Up!
BANANA TURKISH TAFFY
Crack it Up!
STRAWBERRY TURKISH TAFFY
BONOMO
NET WT 1.5 OZ (43g)

Kids loved Turkish Taffy because it could be hard enough to crack into pieces, but would become soft and stretchy if held in a warm hand.

The original Life Savers candy flavors were cherry, orange, lemon, lime and pineapple.

The flavors carry you away

The candy with the hole   ...still only 5¢

WHATEVER KINDS OF COOKIES YOU LIKE...NABISCO BAKES THEM BETTER!

NOW! MORE CREAMY FILLING!
Crumble Oreo between ice-cream layers for a party parfait. The only chocolate sandwich cookie with so much creamy filling between crisp cookies!

NEW OREO CREME SANDWICH

MOIST, LUSCIOUS FIG JAM!
The cookie that goes so well with milk. The fig bar made with the plumpest, juiciest, top-grade figs _exclusively_. Be sure you get the original—

FIG NEWTONS

GOLDEN-CRISP!
Divine in the special banana pudding. (Recipe on the package.) So crisp and light, baked with butter, you'll love them by the handful, too. If you like the _best_—

NABISCO VANILLA WAFERS

BUTTER IN THE BATTER!
Serve 'em with strawberries and cream for a strawberry "short-cut". Shortbread cookies so rich and tender you'll definitely want _only_

LORNA DOONE

Nabisco delivered many famous brands of cookies to our tables, ranging from the rich chocolate flavor of Oreos to the chewy, delicious taste of Fig Newtons.

Cookie Trivia

Q. Which sandwich cookie celebrated its 100th birthday in 2012?

A. Oreos

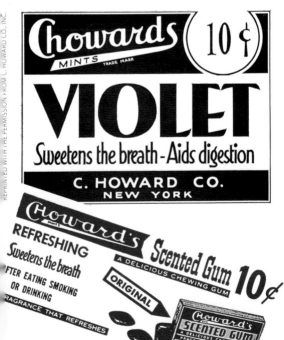

In the early 1930s, Charles Howard started a confectionary company that sold treats with unique flavors and scents.

Chiclets was the original candy-coated gum. Each piece was bursting with fruity flavor.

A Family Line

Here is a list of the dolls created by Mattel in the early years of the Barbie® doll line, the years of production and the relationship of each.

Barbie® 1959–present

Ken® 1961–present
(Barbie doll's boyfriend)

Midge® 1963–1966
(Barbie doll's friend)

Allan® 1964–1965
(Ken doll's friend)

Skipper® 1964–present
(Barbie doll's sister)

Skooter® 1965–1966
(Skipper doll's friend)

Ricky® 1965
(Skipper doll's friend)

The Barbie doll, carrying case and wardrobe pictured on page 31 are all from the collection of *Live It Again's* editor Barb Sprunger, Berne, Ind. BARBIE® and associated trademarks and trade dress are owned by and used with the permission of Mattel, Inc.
© 2012 Mattel, Inc. All rights reserved.

The first Barbie from 1959, shown here, had either blonde or brunette hair with heavy black eyeliner and red lips. She came with a swimsuit, earrings, sunglasses and black heels.

FAMOUS BIRTHDAYS
David Hyde Pierce, April 3 actor
(Niles of *Frasier*)
Emma Thompson, April 15
actress

Barbie® Debuts

Barbie joined the ranks of toy stardom in 1959, delighting girls across America. Barbie was not a baby doll intended to be cuddled, but a fashion doll. Shapely and statuesque in her striped swimming suit and open-toed pumps, the doll introduced by Mattel Inc., sold for $3. The Barbie doll was a redesigned version of a German doll discovered by Ruth Handler, one of the founders of Mattel. The doll was named after her daughter, Barbara. Barbie appealed to preteens who enjoyed imaginative play that revolved around a Barbie world of fashion. The doll was an immediate hit; stores sold more than 300,000 during the first year.

IMAGES ON THIS PAGE WERE PHOTOGRAPHED BY ANNIE'S.

In Barbie's debut year, there were 22 ensembles sold separately. Some of the outfits were casual, but most were glamorous with trendy accessories. The case and Barbie doll above are from 1963 and came with interchangeable wigs.

Two of the separately sold 1959 outfits, Plantation Belle and Suburban Shopper, are shown above.

Dream Toys

For girls

Almost everyone had a special toy as a child. As adults we can revisit our childhood, if only for a little while, by once again seeing, holding or feeling a favorite plaything—whether it's a doll, train or space rocket. The toys featured here and on the following pages were important in the development of our imaginations and creativity.

1959 MONTGOMERY WARD

The lovable characters Raggedy Ann and Andy, Popeye and Dennis the Menace were suitable for all children and ranged in price from $2.29 to $4.98 each.

1959 MONTGOMERY WARD

The mother-daughter look-alike strollers above sold for $18.95 for the pair.

The live action Toddle Trainer doll at right was fully jointed and sold for $9.47. She walked with the use of a metal harness, looking just like a baby taking its first steps.

I'm Toddle Trainer
I WALK WITH YOU

1959 MONTGOMERY WARD

1959 Trivia

Q. Who was Dennis Mitchell's next-door neighbor in the TV show *Dennis the Menace*?

A. George Wilson, played by Joseph Kearns

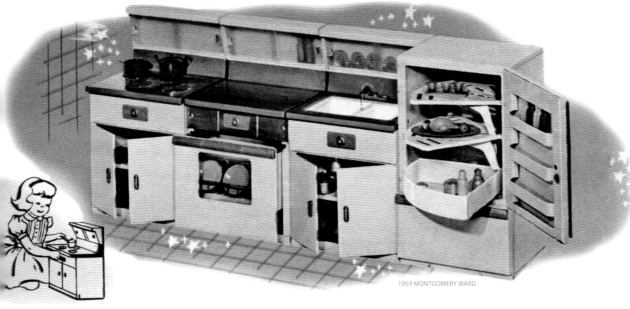

It was a lucky little girl who had this model kitchen to play with. The stove burners lit up, the dishwasher filled with water, and the double sink had a working water faucet. The steel units were priced from $4.97 to $6.97 each.

1959 MONTGOMERY WARD

This four-piece ensemble was styled just like Mother's. Made of fiberboard, the complete set sold for $9.49. The doll wardrobe came with hangers, rod and a top shelf. The vanity featured a real mirror.

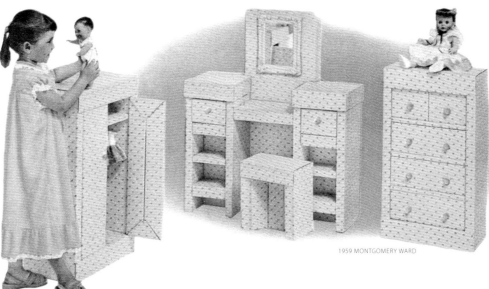

1959 MONTGOMERY WARD

1959 MONTGOMERY WARD

The Betsy McCall doll started out as a paper doll in *McCall's* magazine. Ideal acquired the rights and sold 8-inch plastic dolls for $2.07 and 20-inch dolls for $10.98.

Dream Toys
For boys

The wonderful world of Dr. Seuss expanded from whimsical books to reproduction toys priced from $1.14 to $1.34 each.

Sound and action characterized the Fisher Price toys below. They were sturdily built of wood.

CLANG CLANG

CHUG CHUG

Boys were thrilled with the football outfits above that were made for rough play.

Miniature Magic

For $6.99, this Cape Canaveral rocket research center reproduced the real action with over 100 pieces and launching sounds.

Every child could be a disc jockey with this broadcast outfit that sold for $34.95.

Young Listeners

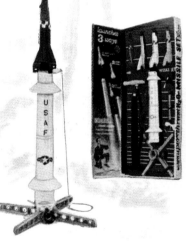

The exciting toy above mimicked combat flight for junior pilots with sound effects and rockets that aimed at moving targets projected on a wall. The missile set, upper right, could be easily launched by air or water pressure.

For $9.88, young musicians could pretend to be Elvis Presley with the working guitar at right.

This teacher demonstrates the sounds letters make while her young students imitate her. The phonics system of teaching reading was often used in 1950s classrooms.

Teachers know their work extends beyond regular school hours and usually welcome parental involvement. At left, this boy is amazingly transformed when the principal is watching.

School Year Memories

When we waved goodbye to our parents that first day of kindergarten, most of us nervously entered the world of learning. Surrounded by a room full of children of the same age, we wondered if we'd be liked by our peers, if the teacher would be kind, or if the food would be tasty. Most important of all, when was recess?

This boy's balancing act is doomed for failure once his teacher puts a stop to his play. Hopefully he will have the presence of mind to give the apples to his instructor to minimize the discipline.

Love is blooming on the jungle gym at recess. The boy is showing off his best climbing skills while the young girl watches in admiration.

"If she knows so much, how come she's only teaching Grade Two?"

School Year Memories

Teen activities

This small town has something to celebrate. The conquering heroes have returned from the big game for their moment of glory.

Band or orchestra was one of the fun classes offered in high school. There was a more relaxed atmosphere where many teens developed a lifetime love of music.

Being part of a school sport taught teamwork. The most common team sports in the 1950s were baseball, football and basketball, though in 1959 wrestling was one of the fastest-growing sports in high schools.

"Oh, good—you met daddy."

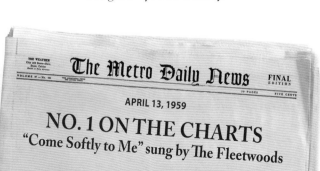

This group of teen girls is being interviewed by the local disc jockey, a memorable occasion for all. Many radio announcers became teen idols.

School Year Memories

Life of a teen girl

The ultimate joy for a teen girl was her very own bedroom. Oh, what bliss to have the privacy and quiet to dream about the future. When a girl had a telephone in her room, she was in teen heaven with peers to call and endless topics to discuss. Life was full and fun with friends to share the good times.

1959 MONTGOMERY WARD

Above, gathering the courage to call a special boy sometimes required the moral support of friends. At right, girls enjoyed collecting record albums of their favorite artists.

1959 MONTGOMERY WARD

Record totes, diaries and photo albums were popular gifts for teen girls. The "clever" cloth puppies at left were intended for signatures of friends.

A roomful of pillows was a comfy spot for those long phone conversations. The pillows with captions were called "wise-guy" pillows. They were designed for laughs as well as comfort.

"These are all the beauty aids my sister needs, and she's only 23. Sort of frightens you, doesn't it?"

How fun it was to decorate your own room with things that proclaimed your personal sense of style with desk sets, scrapbooks or a personalized bulletin board.

What Made Us Laugh

"I like you, son—it's just that we feel our
refrigerator is too young to go steady."

"Feeling tired, listless and thoroughly worn out?
Why not switch me off and go to bed?"

"It's been taken care of by the gentleman."

"Which do you think will be more appropriate, dear—my tweed with frayed cuffs or my navy with the moth holes?"

"I believe he's the senior partner. I wouldn't ask him to recommend any low-priced sleepers."

"The money we just saved, Ella—do you have any idea where we can borrow it?"

Lee Petty poses with his trophy after winning the Daytona 500. The finish was too close to call until three days after the race, when newsreel footage was viewed.

Rodger Ward won the 1959 Indianapolis 500 with an average speed of 135.857 mph.

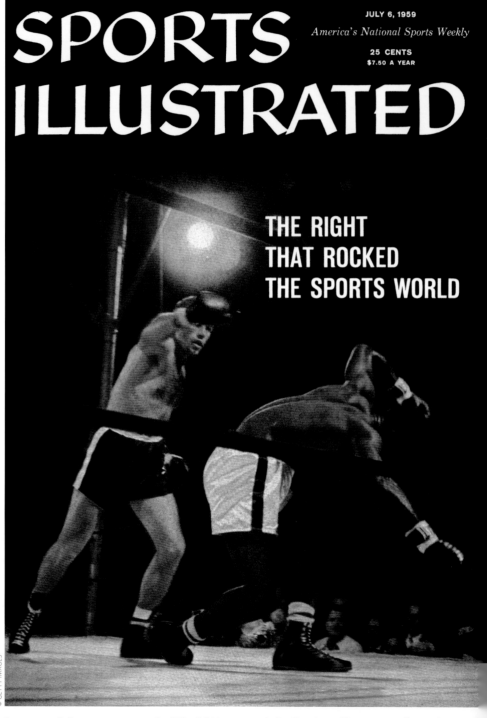

JULY 6, 1959
America's National Sports Weekly

25 CENTS
$7.50 A YEAR

SPORTS ILLUSTRATED

THE RIGHT
THAT ROCKED
THE SPORTS WORLD

Ingemar Johansson won the World Heavyweight Boxing Championship when he defeated Floyd Patterson by technical knockout in the third round. In 1959 he was named the Associated Press Male Athlete of the Year and *Sports Illustrated* magazine's Sportsman of the Year.

Sporting Champions

The Boston Celtics, under the leadership of coach Red Auerbach, swept the NBA Finals in four games to begin a string of consecutive championships that lasted through 1966. They defeated the Minneapolis Lakers who managed to keep every game close, but couldn't produce a win.

The sport of automobile racing had its share of thrills in 1959. On Feb. 22, the very first Daytona 500 was won by Lee Petty, who collected about $68,000 in prize money. Petty was one of the pioneers of NASCAR. On May 23, Rodger Ward won the Indianapolis 500 at the famed Brickyard. He said, "Winning that race was the greatest thing that happened to me in my life."

The Boston Celtics, NBA champions, pose for a team photo. Coach Red Auerbach, front row holding the ball, created a unique team atmosphere with a mixture of toughness and fun.

© GETTY IMAGES

Sporting Champions

Golfer Art Wall Jr., above, was chosen as the PGA Player of the year. He won the Masters Tournament in dramatic fashion, coming from five strokes behind to capture the victory. Betsy Rawls, upper right, didn't start golfing until age 17, though it wasn't long until she was one of the top women's players. In 1959 she won the LPGA Championship.

Alex Olmedo, born and raised in Peru, was the top amateur tennis player in 1959. He won both the Wimbledon and Australian singles titles.

The Orange Bowl, Miami, Fla., was the setting for one of college football's popular bowl games. What began in 1935 as a game that drew only about 5,000 people grew into an elaborate production that packed the large stadium in 1959 for Oklahoma's defeat of Duke, 48-21.

Racehorse owner Isabel Dodge Sloane is shown with her horse, Sword Dancer, after victory in the Belmont Stakes. The horse was voted 1959 U.S. Horse of the Year. Well-known jockey Willie Shoemaker sits in the saddle. A small man, his size proved to be an asset in horse racing, leading to a record number of professional career victories.

1959 Trivia

Q. Who won the 1959 U.S. Women's Open?

A. Mickey Wright

Sporting Champions

The 1959 NFL championship game was played on December 27 at Memorial Stadium in Baltimore, Md., a rematch of the 1958 championship game. The Baltimore Colts were again victorious over the New York Giants, 31-16. Left, Baltimore Colts quarterback Johnny Unitas prepares to hand off the ball during a play. He is often referred to as one of the greatest NFL players of all time. Above, Gene Lipscomb, No. 76 of the Colts, takes a break while head coach Weeb Ewbank, far right, concentrates on game play. Ewbank was the only coach to lead teams from both the National and American Football leagues to the NFL championship.

© 1959 SE

© GETTY IMAGES

World Series

1959
OFFICIAL PROGRAM
50¢

Chicago
WHITE SOX

The Los Angeles Dodgers defeated the Chicago White Sox, four games to two, to bring home the World Series Championship. It was the first pennant for the team since moving from Brooklyn in 1958. This was also the first World Series since 1948 with no games played in New York City. Dodger pitcher Larry Sherry was the series MVP. At left, Wally Moon and Duke Snider of the Dodgers collided and dropped the ball during game one.

1959
WORLD SERIES
NATIONAL LEAGUE
VS.
AMERICAN LEAGUE
LOS ANGELES COLISEUM

RESERVED
GAME
3

$7.00

Do not detach
this coupon from
RAIN CHECK

Los Angeles Dodgers
1959
WORLD SERIES
LOS ANGELES COLISEUM
National League
VS.
American League

RAIN CHECK
ADMIT ONE
Subject to the conditions
set forth on back hereof
FORD C. FRICK
Commissioner

GAME
3

RESERVED
16
STAR
58
ROW
104
SEAT

EST. PR. $6.45
FED. TAX .55
$7.00

The victorious 1959 Los Angeles Dodgers, above, pose for a team photo. The excited fans, at left, cheer for the winning team.

The Ford Country Squire was a 9-passenger station wagon. Priced at $3,076, it ran on regular gas that saved money.

The Car Review

Auto industry sales for 1959 surpassed those of 1958 by nearly 2 million units. Though statistics indicated the public still wanted a big car, the success of small cars such as the Rambler and Studebaker-Packard's Lark made the "Big Three," Chrysler, Ford and GM, take notice. The companies tooled up for production of small cars to be on the road by year's end.

Advertisements for the Chevrolet Nomad station wagon emphasized the slim-line design and sweeping new curved windshield.

59 FORDS are built for people
59 FORDS are built for savings

The Ford Thunderbird sold for $2,707. It featured a finish the manufacturer claimed never needed waxing!

HAVE A LARK—SAVE A LOT
WITH THE PERFECT ONE FOR WORK 'N' FUN
THE LARK *PLAY WAGON BY STUDEBAKER*

Studebaker's Lark Play Wagon, priced at $2,295, was shorter outside than most other station wagons which made it easier to park, turn and handle.

Here's how your family will find out . . .
IT PAYS
TO OWN A DODGE

RANCHER GETS BUM STEER by Griffith

"I need a vacation," said the Texas cattle-king. "Why not get yourself a big new car," said his foreman, "pack up your family, and visit New York?"

So he did. But by the time he reached the Texas border, the big car had burned up all his cash in gas and oil and repairs. So he had to hock his guns and spurs.

In the big city, they found the big bus wouldn't fit regular parking spaces, and garages charged double. "Looks like I got a bum steer," said the Texan.

He tried a little foreign car, but there wasn't room for his size-12 boots and 20-gallon hat. "Where," asked his wife, "would the kiddies ride . . . sidesaddle?"

Then, a friendly native spoke up: "Try Rambler, with big-car room, small-car economy." So they did . . . and had a fine time seeing the town in this easier-handling car.

With front seats that glide back and forth individually, the tall Texan had extra legroom. Low-cost air conditioning kept them cool on the desert. Try it.

Go Rambler...*the compact* quality car*
Get the best of both: Big car room, small car economy

A 1959 Dodge with a V-8 engine delivered about 22 mpg for gas economy.

The Car Review
Cool convertibles

The Pontiac convertible above was the only car with wide-track wheels—five inches more than the average car.

Buick claimed its cars averaged 15–18 mpg from the best engines the company had built to date.

The 1959 Plymouth was deliberately designed with flair, yet restraint. "For good taste in cars is neither stodgy nor bizarre," the advertisement proclaimed.

lion-hearted
CHRYSLER
...setting the pace in style and comfort

SWEET TEMPTATION
...your lion-hearted '59 Chrysler!

Selling for $4,890, the Chrysler New Yorker convertible featured the ease of an optional swivel seat.

Ford's Sunliner convertible had wide doors. The ad stated that the car could go 4,000 miles without an oil change.

Car Promo Quiz

Match the promotional text given in the featured advertisement with the car model.

1. The smart way to go places.
2. Excellence without equal.
3. The world's most eloquent possession.
4. America's number 1 road car!
5. Get the best of both: big car room, small car economy.
6. Today's best buy, tomorrow's best trade.

A. Pontiac
B. Rambler
C. Imperial
D. De Soto
E. Plymouth
F. Cadillac

Answers: 1-D; 2-C; 3-F; 4-A; 5-B; 6-E.

The Car Review

Luxury autos

The Cadillac DeVille Sedan sold for $5,498. The car was known for luxury, refinement and fine craftsmanship.

Swing in...stretch out

REVEL IN CHRYSLER ROOMINESS!

The world's most eloquent possession... *Cadillac*

lion-hearted **CHRYSLER**
...setting the pace in style and comfort

Priced at $3,353, the Chrysler Windsor had swivel seats, the latest in comfort.

The Chrysler Imperial LeBaron, right, had auto-pilot to hold the speed steady on long trips. This was a top-of-the-line car that cost $6,389.

The Metro Daily News

FINAL EDITION

MAY 12, 1959

ELIZABETH TAYLOR WEDS EDDIE FISHER

This is Liz's fourth marriage and Eddie's second.

IMPERIAL
...excellence without equal
FINEST PRODUCT OF CHRYSLER CORPORATION

OLDSMOBILE

SUPER 88 HOLIDAY SCENICOUPE

The trim, modern style of the 1959 Oldsmobile was an invitation to get out and go.

BLESS DE SOTO

for making seats that let you step out like a lady!

The smart way to go places... DE SOTO

A Buick was a quality car with power steering and a new automatic heat and fresh-air control.

PONTIAC! America's Number ① Road Car!

The Pontiac Bonneville featured wide-track wheels and had a unique grille. The selling price was $3,333.

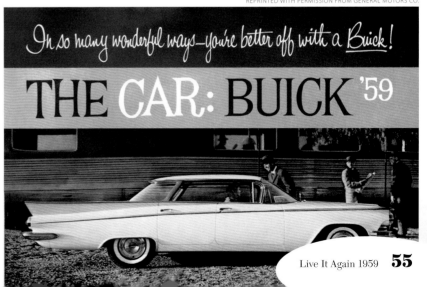

In so many wonderful ways—you're better off with a Buick!

THE CAR: BUICK '59

INTRODUCING
EDSEL FOR 1960

The Edsel was intended for people who enjoyed luxury, yet wanted economy.

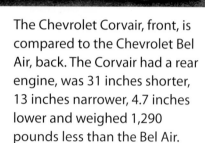

The Chevrolet Corvair, front, is compared to the Chevrolet Bel Air, back. The Corvair had a rear engine, was 31 inches shorter, 13 inches narrower, 4.7 inches lower and weighed 1,290 pounds less than the Bel Air.

A wonderful new world of savings in the New-size FORD

The Ford Falcon got up to 30 miles a gallon on regular gas and held six passengers for an economical $1,974.

THE NEW 1960 *Ford Falcon*

FORD DIVISION, *Ford Motor Company*

The Car Review

Looking ahead to 1960

What did a new decade—the 1960s—hold for future car buyers? The American auto industry planned for better small cars to meet the increasing demand. The public seemed to like these reduced-size autos that had room for families, but were easier on the pocketbook. General Motors, Ford and Chevrolet, the manufacturers who represented 90 percent of American car production, were ready for the style revolution. These new cars were more nimble and gas efficient. Unfortunately, only a limited number of the new models could be made due to the steel strike, the longest in history to date. So for the time being, larger cars were still the standard.

The Lark, made by Studebaker, was the first full line of new small cars. They featured glowing colors and saved money on insurance and mileage.

REPRINTED WITH PERMISSION FROM GENERAL MOTORS CO.

The 1960 Oldsmobile was for people who wanted the finest car available in the medium-price class, with prices ranging from $2,900 to $3,325.

ENTER! IMPERIAL 1960

COURTESY OF CHRYSLER GROUP LLC

The completely new Chrysler Imperial handled as if it were a thousand pounds lighter than it actually weighed. The emphasis was still on quality, comfort and space. It sold for $4,956.

PRINTED WITH PERMISSION OF STUDEBAKER NATIONAL MUSEUM

E THAT
LARK
BY STUDEBAKER

FAMOUS BIRTHDAYS
Jenilee Harrison, June 12 actress (Cindy Snow of *Three's Company*)
Vincent D'Onofrio, June 30 actor (Det. Robert Goren of *Law & Order: Criminal Intent*)

A Year With President Eisenhower

In 1959, President Dwight D. Eisenhower was named "Man of the Year" by *Time* magazine. *Time* said, "He has personally revitalized the image of America throughout the world, and given the United States a new understanding of its mission, role and challenge in the world."

Eisenhower's top priority for the year was to find ways to a peaceful Russian-American coexistence. He also worked to strengthen the West's defenses in Europe. On the domestic front, he proposed a balanced budget of about $77 million. The president's health proved to be equal to his full travel schedule and the demands of the office.

Made by Crosley, this Runabout, at right, had "Ike" and "Mamie" stenciled on the front quarter panels. The vehicle, a gift, had four-wheel drive and was used by the Eisenhowers to drive around their Gettysburg farm. In this photo, the president takes Winston Churchill, seated on Ike's right, on a tour.

Mamie Eisenhower reflected the general values, roles and priorities of middle class American women in the areas of style, family, home and entertaining during her time in the White House.

President Eisenhower speaks at a press conference. Ike was at the top of the annual Gallup poll on "the most admired man in the world" for the seventh straight year.

Gospel singer Mahalia Jackson, far left, performed for the president and gave him an album of her records. Soviet Premier Nikita Khrushchev, right, met with the president in 1959. One of Eisenhower's greatest presidential accomplishments was his successful efforts to keep America at peace during the Cold War.

Alaska has more than three million lakes, including Wonder Lake, shown above, with Mount McKinley in the background.

COURTESY OF THE DWIGHT D. EISENHOWER PRESIDENTIAL LIBRARY & MUSEUM; NPS PHOTO 72-2933-2

U.S. Trivia

Q. Which were the last two contiguous states to be added to the Union?

A. New Mexico and Arizona in 1912

© GETTY IMAGES
WIKIMEDIA PUBLIC DOMAIN PHOTOGRAPH

Hawaii's beautiful scenery, warm climate, active volcanoes and public beaches continue to make it a popular tourist destination.

President Eisenhower and other onlookers smile as the flag with 49 stars in honor of Alaska's statehood is raised. Alaskans had longed to be part of the Union for many years and rejoiced when they were able to send delegates to Congress.

Alaska and Hawaii Become States

Two more states were added to the Union in 1959, making it a historically significant year for the United States. The drive to include Alaska and Hawaii was chiefly due to their locations and a result of World War II and the Cold War security concerns.

On January 3, Alaska was the first of the two states to officially be added to "the lower 48." It became the largest state with a longer coastline than all the other U.S. states combined. Alaska contributed to the energy resources of the country with its large oil and gas reserves.

Hawaii, the only U.S. state made up entirely of islands, was officially proclaimed the 50th state on August 21. The presidential action was followed by the unveiling of the new fifty-star flag. More than 3,000 people had sent in their ideas for the updated design. An *Alaska Anchorage Daily Times* headline read, "Aloha, Hawaii: You're In Too."

Hawaiians of all ages celebrated statehood with bonfires, horns honking and dancing in the streets.

COURTESY OF THE DWIGHT D. EISENHOWER PRESIDENTIAL LIBRARY & MUSEUM, NPS PHOTO 77-18-1154

Congratulatory handshakes are offered as Hawaii is admitted as the 50th state. Seated is President Eisenhower, and to the left is Vice President Nixon.

THE WEATHER
City and State—Fair,
Dept. Cooler

The Metro Daily News

VOLUME 87—No. 193

FINAL EDITION

35 PAGES

FIVE CENTS

JUNE 1, 1959

NO. 1 ON THE CHARTS
"The Battle of New Orleans"
sung by Johnny Horton

Front-Page News

U.S. happenings

Among the notable headlines of 1959 was the news that steelworkers had gone on strike on July 15, an act that shut down 90 percent of U.S. steel production. The strike was part of a sweep of labor unrest during the year that included a walkout of autoworkers. On October 19, President Eisenhower ordered the steelworkers back to work through the Taft-Harley Act.

The St. Lawrence Seaway, a system of locks and canals that extends from Montreal to Lake Erie, was a project jointly undertaken by the United States and Canada. The engineering miracle that could accommodate large ocean liners officially opened for business on June 26. President Eisenhower and Queen Elizabeth, who was on a tour of Canada, both attended the event, as pictured on the facing page.

Members of the United Steelworkers of America picket outside a steel plant. The strike was settled in January of 1960, with wage concessions made by the companies.

U.S. News

United Steelworkers Strike

Guggenheim Museum Opens in New York City

St. Lawrence Seaway Dedicated

Crowds of people gather in New York City for the opening of the Guggenheim Museum. The last of Frank Lloyd Wright's designs, this building included spiral galleries.

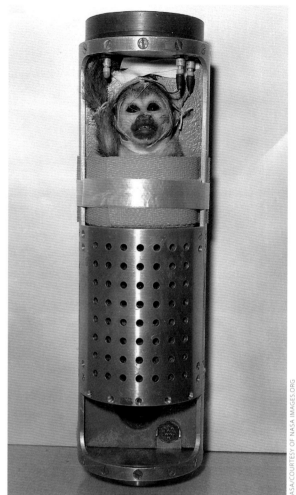

On May 28, 1959, NASA sent two monkeys, Able and Baker, into space to test the safety of human space travel. Baker, above, is being readied for the 16-minute flight in the capsule.

On March 3, 1959, the Juno II launch vehicle, shown above, was used to send the Pioneer 4 satellite to the moon.

The Metro Daily News

FINAL EDITION

JULY 28, 1959

ATLAS ICBM TEST ROCKET LAUNCH FROM CAPE CANAVERAL, FLA. IS SUCCESSFUL

The previous three attempts exploded mid-flight.

Front-Page News

Advancements in space

The exploration of space taught us to view the universe and the earth in new ways. Fueled with a $145 million budget, the best of NASA's engineers readied the Juno II rocket to carry the Pioneer 4 satellite to the moon. The satellite escaped earth's gravitational pull and returned data on the radiation in the moon's environment.

In April, NASA announced the names of the first astronauts who would be sent into space. The seven men went on to become national heroes as they blazed the trail for future space travelers.

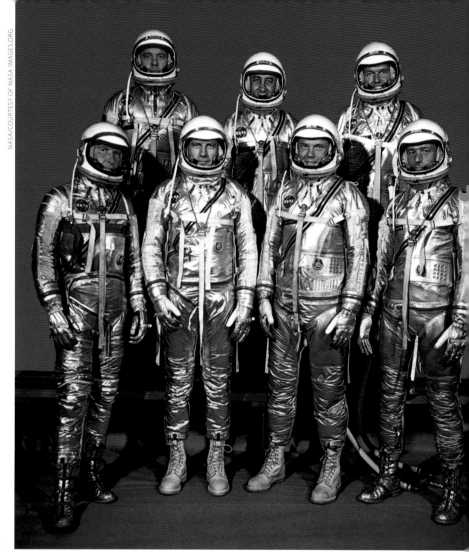

NASA/COURTESY OF NASA IMAGES.ORG

Pictured are the original seven astronauts selected in 1959 for Project Mercury. They are, left to right in front, Wally Schirra, Deke Slayton, John Glenn Jr. and Scott Carpenter. Shown left to right at rear are Alan Shepard, Gus Grissom and Gordon Cooper Jr.

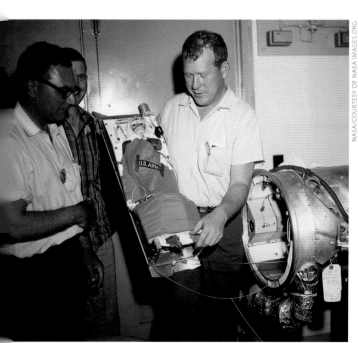

NASA/COURTESY OF NASA IMAGES.ORG

The monkey Abel is shown just before the NASA test flight on May 28. Both Able and Baker returned from their space adventure in good condition.

Space Trivia

Q. Which one of the original astronauts shown on this page walked on the moon?

A. Alan Shepard in 1971

Front-Page News

World events

In 1959, Tibet rebelled against Chinese rule in their territory. Tibet's political and spiritual head, the Dalai Lama, managed to escape the country, dressed as a Chinese soldier and aided by a blinding sandstorm. The escape party wound its way through the Himalayan Mountains toward India with the Chinese in hot pursuit. One observer said it was one of the most remarkable escapes in history.

Fidel Castro and his band of soldiers took control of Cuba's government, shocking the world. It seemed impossible to many that a small guerrilla army could overthrow Dictator Fulgencio Batista and his 10,000 troops.

Near McMurdo Station, Antarctica, a driller extracts a core of ice that holds clues to the past climate. Twelve countries, including the U.S., signed a historic international agreement to save Antarctica. Military bases were banned, but scientists of all nations were allowed free access to carry out research and study the wildlife.

Fidel Castro, above, triumphantly made his way to Havana, seizing control of the Cuban government.

In July of 1959, anthropologists Mary and Louis Leakey were working in Tanzania. They discovered "Nutcracker Man," an early ancestor of humans, shocking the scientific community. Up to that time, the oldest remains were those of "Peking Man," found in China and about 500,000 years old. The Leakeys' find was dated at 1.75 million years, indicating that Africa, not Asia, was the birthplace of human evolution.

World News

Outstanding Events

Castro Takes Control of Cuba

The Dalai Lama Escapes to India

Archaeologists Unearth Ancient Human Remains

Antarctica Is Saved

The Dalai Lama, leader of Tibet, flees with his warrior guards following a failed uprising against Chinese occupation. After a two-week ordeal, the party managed to reach safety in India.

What Made Us Laugh

"I understand you just came back from Cape Canaveral."

"It's their lunch hour."

"Now if you can give me a few bucks to have it framed."

"What I said was, 'Don't open the door.'"

"What happened to the friendly
little club we used to have?"

"Just how am I supposed to figure this out?"

"Dawson, I don't like to interfere in
your domestic problems, but ...."

"It's the only way I can get
him to take his medicine."

Understated elegance was Chanel's hallmark. Custom-made to the client's measurements, the average Chanel required about 150 hours of hand stitching at a cost of about $500. The average number of original Chanel designs was limited to about 1,800 a year.

FAMOUS BIRTHDAYS

Gary Anderson, July 16 NFL placekicker (Pittsburgh Steelers, Minnesota Vikings)

Kevin Spacey, July 26 actor (*American Beauty*)

Fashionable Clothing

Stylish designs

Coco Chanel, a well-known fashion designer, was born in France in 1883. Her trademarks were her timeless designs, trim suits and little black dresses. In the 1920s she launched her first perfume, Chanel No. 5. She was an admired style icon known for her simple yet sophisticated outfits paired with great accessories, such as several strands of pearls. She retired in 1938, and then made a triumphant return to the fashion world in 1954. Her feminine yet easy-fitting designs drew shoppers from around the world.

MEMORABLE QUOTE

"Of course, most women dress for men and want to be admired. But also, they must be able to move, to get into a car, to do this, that, without bursting a seam. Clothes must be natural!"

—Coco Chanel

Designer Coco Chanel, above left, also known for her famous Chanel No. 5 perfume, returned to the fashion world when she was in her mid-seventies to restore comfort to designer clothing.

The new Coco Chanel look emphasized youth, simplicity and ease. The clothes she designed "walked with the girl" with "give" around the hips, incorporating the idea of "enough, and not too much."

Fashionable Clothing

For women

Women's fashions became more figure-defining with the return of belted waistlines in a move the fashion world called a "return to normal." The reliable shirtwaist dress was popular in 1959, with most women choosing to keep their knees covered by about two inches of fabric.

The pleats of the dress at left were crease-resistant and needed little ironing when drip dried.

The shirtwaist dress, left, cost $5.98. The lightweight tapestry coat below was priced at $19.98.

1959 MONTGOMERY WARD

© 1959 SEPS

1959 MONTGOMERY WARD

1959 MONTGOMERY WARD

1959 MONTGOMERY WARD

"This one is a wonderful buy if madame has a sense of humor."

These women were ready for the beach scene with a figure-molding swimsuit, fashionable rubber swim cap and capri-length pants.

Above, wool-mohair blend was the season's most luxurious coat fabric.

Bright red and olive green were declared the college-girls' favorite colors. The sleeveless dresses above, priced at $7.98, were called "patio cottons." The Dacron blends at right were easy to care for and cost from $10.98 to $14.98.

The new colors, above, were taken straight from the palette of fashion's premier hues in linen-like fabrics.

Fashionable Clothing
Trendy accents

Eyewear of 1959 had fashion flair. Colors and styles could be chosen to enhance the face, keeping in mind complexion, hairstyle, facial features, and of course, eyes.

FAMOUS BIRTHDAYS
Rosanna Arquette, August 10
actress (*Desperately Seeking Susan*)
Magic Johnson, August 14
basketball player (Los Angeles Lakers)

Accessories were carefully coordinated with fashions for a polished look. The three-compartment handbag above cost $8.50; the 16-strand necklace was $2.87. The shoes featured reversible bows for versatility. The hat was called a tucked-down cloche.

The jewelry, handbag and airy mesh pumps with 3-inch heels were lovely accessories. The "hint of a tint" nylons were available in rust, smoke, sapphire, midnight and blush.

The hats above, priced at $7.98 and $5.98, were flattering and feminine.

The hat, leather bag, strappy pumps and rhinestone jewelry above added sparkle and sophistication to everyday outfits.

The straw handbag, silk scarf, sandals and pearlized glass-bead jewelry above were just right for warm-weather wear.

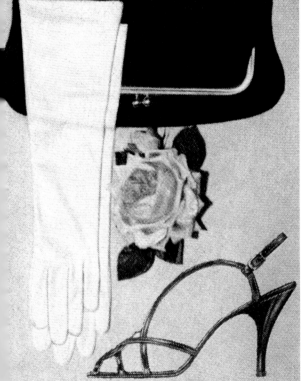

"Here's something clever—it has a zipper in the bottom for those little hard-to-get-at things."

A woman would turn heads dressed in the accessories at left. The mink stole was sale-priced at $299, a temptation for the fashionable woman of the 1950s.

Fashionable Clothing

Shopping for girls

Fashions were changing for girls. Dresses could be worn with or without belts for versatility. White bobby socks and patent-leather shoes, though, remained popular for dress-up occasions.

Two-Way Dres

WEAR IT LOOSE OR BELTED

The bright solid and print coordinates, upper left, cost from $1.59 to $1.98. Pop Tops, left, were the new rage for girls ages 7–14. They could be worn two ways with a different print on each side.

An appliquéd poodle and a kerchief enhance the full skirts above. The two-piece sets at right cost from $3.98 to $4.95 each.

It was still fun for sisters to dress alike, especially during the holidays. Perfect for church and parties, these velveteen and nylon dresses were styled with the charm girls loved.

Fun robes of quilted cotton had bell sleeves, pert bows and side pockets, priced at $3.98 and $4.98.

Bulky knit sweaters that were embroidered with yuletide poinsettias were perfect Christmas gifts for girls.

Fashionable Clothing

Shopping for boys

Wash-and-wear fabrics were popular, as was the color red. The shirts at right were $2.98 and $1.98. The heavy-weight hooded sweatshirt, lower right, was lined in cotton fleece for warmth.

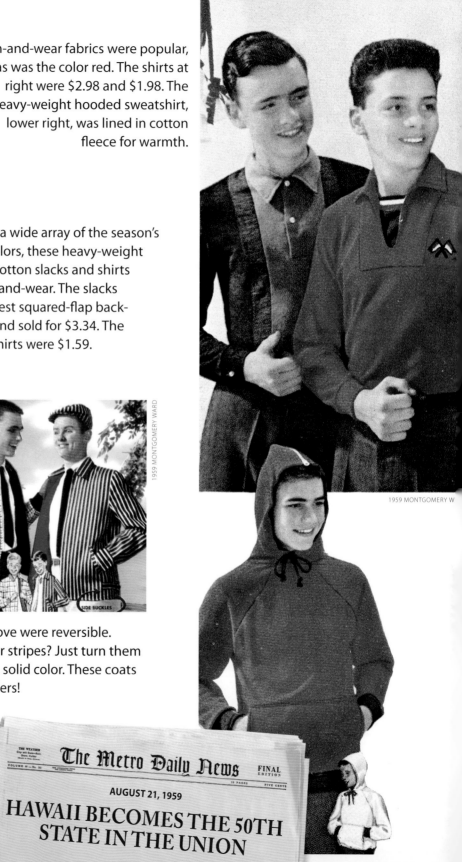

1959 MONTGOMERY WARD

1959 MONTGOMERY W

Available in a wide array of the season's newest colors, these heavy-weight polished cotton slacks and shirts were wash-and-wear. The slacks had the newest squared-flap back-pocket style and sold for $3.34. The coordinating shirts were $1.59.

Wash'n'Wear

LITTLE OR NO IRONING

1959 MONTGOMERY WARD

SIDE BUCKLES

1959 MONTGOMERY WARD

The jackets above were reversible. Tired of plaid or stripes? Just turn them inside out for a solid color. These coats were style leaders!

THE WEATHER

The Metro Daily News

FINAL EDITION

AUGUST 21, 1959

HAWAII BECOMES THE 50TH STATE IN THE UNION

The washable heavy-weight sweaters, left, were warm and stylish. They ranged in price from $3.89 to $4.89 each.

The boldly printed pajamas, below, were made of cotton flannel. They ranged in price from $2.29 to $2.98 for each pair.

Smart outfits included bold plaids and stripes. The matching flannel slacks were called "longies." The outfits were $9.98 each.

Fashionable Clothing
The look for men

1959 MONTGOMERY WARD

THE ARROW MARK IS USED WITH THE PERMISSION OF PVH CORP.

Arrow wash-and-wear shirts were ideal for travel. The fabric was comfortable, and the shirt stayed neat, even without ironing. The shirts were $4.25, and the all-silk ties were $2.50.

The fleece suburban coat at right was tailored like a topcoat with many extras for finer fit. It was priced at $21.50.

REPRINTED WITH PERMISSION FROM BOTANY 500

the 'Botany' *500 look*

as tailored by Daroff

the greatest summer fashion is the cool comfort of the lightest 2-Ply Tropical ever!

'SPECTACULAR' 2/80's . . . $65

Its secret of cool, unwrinkled comfort is in the world's rarest worsted yarns skillfully blended with Dacron.* The secret of the 'Botany' '500' look of importance and success is in the Daroff tailoring, and the impeccable good taste of correct colors and smart fashion. The expertly combined comfort and flattery is your in America's greatest summer clothing value. Prices slightly higher in the West

*DuPont trademark for polyester fiber

BOTANY 500 | Look for the *complete* wardrobe with this label.

'BOTANY' '500'
tailored by DAROFF

at your nearest 'BOTANY' '500' *dealer or write:*
H. DAROFF & SONS, Inc., 200 Fifth Avenue, New York 10, N. Y. • 2300 Walnut Street, Philadelphia 3, Pa.

The Metro Daily News

THE WEATHER
City and State—Rain,
Snow, Colder,
March 4 cloudy

VOLUME 87—No. 261

FINAL
EDITION

20 PAGES   FIVE CENTS

SEPTEMBER 12, 1959

BONANZA DEBUTS ON NBC
This is the first Western TV show to be televised in color.

These trim Jarman shoes were smart, snug and comfortable. This shade of brown went well not only with brown and tan, but also many shades of gray and blue.

The men's accessories, above, were coordinated for a finished look. The wool-lined leather gloves were $5.98. The cap and muffler sold as a set for $5.

"Notice how it fits over the shoulders!"

Men were at the height of fashion when dressed in the cabana sets, shorts and shirts at left. They were easy-care and allowed freedom of movement.

The neighborhood kids are armed and ready to attack anyone brave enough to pass their fortress. This dad is wisely considering his options.

Papa is slumped down in his chair, hoping to not be noticed by his church-going family, though the scattered newspapers give him away.

A fun family boating outing goes awry when the gas supply runs out. Good thing there's an oar. Dad will be getting a workout!

TV Dad Quiz

Match the actor with the TV role he played in 1959.

1. Desi Arnaz
2. Robert Young
3. Herbert Anderson
4. Hugh Beaumont
5. Chuck Connors
6. Jon Shepodd
7. Lorne Greene

A. Henry Mitchell of *Dennis the Menace*
B. Paul Martin of *Lassie*
C. Ricky Ricardo of *I Love Lucy*
D. Ben Cartwright of *Bonanza*
E. Ward Cleaver of *Leave It to Beaver*
F. Lucas McCain of *The Rifleman*
G. Jim Anderson of *Father Knows Best*

Answers: 1-C; 2-G; 3-A; 4-E; 5-F; 6-B; 7-D

Through a Father's Eyes

A father loves to be the conquering hero, the one who manages to smooth over life's rough spots for his loving family. Sometimes his efforts backfire, though. Oh, the embarrassment of being caught in imperfection! A papa's work is never done.

This father loves his womenfolk dearly but is clearly dismayed by the price tag that goes along with making them happy.

Dad—what a guy! Mom will be forever grateful that he found the missing silverware, even though it meant digging through the trash in the dark.

The family arrives for a weekend ski trip, ready to enjoy the slopes, when rain begins to fall. Dad is pondering ways to salvage the vacation.

Challenges of Motherhood

A sense of humor goes a long way toward making the occasional trials and tribulations of being a mother more bearable. Besides, moms will later laugh long and hard about some of the more outrageous of their children's shenanigans. Children may be embarrassed by the stories mothers tell, but laughing together adds such joy to life.

A snowman mysteriously appears in the freezer, scaring a few years off Mom's life.

"I want my mother!"

Mom is concentrating so hard on her son's hair that she doesn't know he's blowing a bubble large enough to mess up his face and clothes for the annual photo.

When the woman at left was single and working in a tidy office, she daydreamed about finding the perfect man, one who would regularly send her flowers. After marriage, she's up to her elbows in dirty dishes and longing for her previous office job.

The kids are off to school at last, and Mom has earned her time of rest.

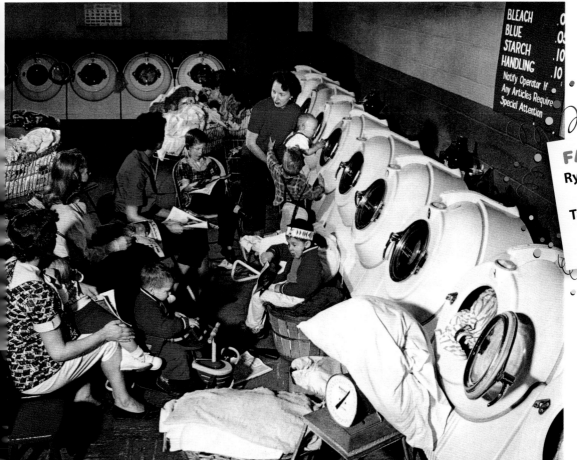

FAMOUS BIRTHDAYS

Ryne Sandberg, September 18
second baseman (Chicago Cubs)

Tai Babilonia, September 22
five-time U.S. pairs figure skating champion

The young mothers, left, turn the routine of doing laundry into a social gathering. The kids play, the latest gossip is exchanged, and tips on raising children are shared.

Why would such a harmless-looking pair of grandmothers be trying to stay out of the hands of the cops? They thought they were speeding, but the policeman was just trying to do them a favor.

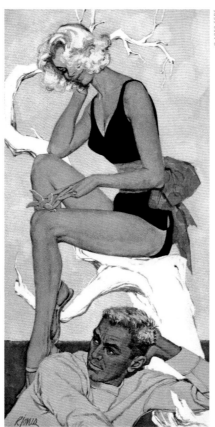

He wanted the job, but not if he had to marry the boss's daughter.

FAMOUS BIRTHDAYS
Simon Cowell, October 7 TV personality (*American Idol* judge)
Marie Osmond, October 13 country musician (*Donny and Marie Show*)
Emeril Lagasse, October 15 chef, TV show host, restaurateur

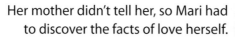

Her mother didn't tell her, so Mari had to discover the facts of love herself.

Leading Ladies of *The Post*

Take a peek at some of the art inside the covers of *The Saturday Evening Post*. The Leading Ladies of *The Post* are a collection of images from regularly featured steamy romance stories. Illustrators were challenged to interpret these stories on canvas, and we have included a sampling of the Leading Ladies of 1959. The sultry, fashion-forward heroines of the tales are featured along with the original article captions.

She had such expensive tastes. How could any man afford her? "The best things in life," he said softly, "are free."

He had a weakness for women—and her job was to exploit it.

Sometimes a dance can be the turning point of a girl's life.

Looking for Love

A *Reader's Digest* article on dating listed the proper etiquette for spending time with the opposite sex in the 1950s. The girls were reminded that only floozies ask guys out. Don't humiliate guys by trying to pay for a date, ladies! Guys were advised that real gentlemen open car doors for girls and don't kiss on the first date.

In this case, the athlete doesn't attract the girls. These young ladies are more interested in a guy's potential to be successful in the working world.

"I'll remember this night long after you repay the 10 dollars I loaned you for dinner!"

This couple has been an item for some time, and she is hoping he will pop the question. He is likely trying to come up with just the right words to do the asking.

When a guy is interested in a girl, he'll wisely escort her anywhere she desires, even if it's a Shakespeare festival.

He was planning to impress her with his sailing technique, but instead he's seasick while she's having the time of her life!

Drive-in movies were a popular date activity in the 1950s. Maybe this couple will be sitting a little closer by the time the film draws to a close.

This ad shows that 7UP is the perfect drink to energize and put the sparkle back in her eyes after an embarrassing fall.

Forever Smart, So Young at Heart

Elegance, grace, trimness of line—these describe the look of today's America and its people. For the new light look is everywhere, engaging and flattering.

Move toward the light look. Look smart. Stay young and fair and debonair. Be sociable. Have a Pepsi—the lighter Pepsi of today, reduced in calories.

PEPSI-COLA

Even Pepsi Cola used the 1950s fascination with wedded bliss to sell their product.

A bride-to-be could order dresses for the wedding from the Montgomery Ward catalog or shop at the store in person.

CELEBRITY WEDDINGS OF 1959

Julie London and Bobby Troup

Eva Gabor and Richard Brown

Glen Campbell and Billie Jean Nunley

Margaret O'Brien and Harold Allen Jr.

Peter Finch and Yolande Turner

Dorothy Malone and Jacques Bergerac

Eddie Fisher and Elizabeth Taylor

Julie Andrews and Tony Walton

Barbara Billingsley and William Mortensen

James Coburn and Beverly Kelly

Tammy Wynette and Euple Byrd

Donald Sutherland and Lois Hardwick

A wedding day is also a special event for the mothers of the bride and groom. They want to look their very best for the milestone event

Looking for Love

Saying "I do"

From the moment the engagement became a fact, life was full of activities for the bride of 1959. First, her beau had to get up the nerve to ask her father for permission to marry her. Then he presented her with a perfect diamond ring. Her parents may have announced her engagement at a party and publically in the newspapers. Then it was time to prepare for the wedding itself to ensure a memorable occasion.

A final glance in the mirror assures this bride she is picture-perfect for her wedding.

A DIAMOND IS FOREVER

"I think it's going to get interesting now."

An engagement diamond mirrors a couple's dreams and happiness with sparkle and shine.

The numbered map circles labeled 1 through 12.

Vacation Adventures

We were off to see the sights in 1959. With jets linking the United States to more parts of the world, 1.5 million Americans chose to vacation overseas. France and Italy were the top destinations. Hawaii and Alaska, riding on the wave of statehood, drew many visitors. Popular locations for trips in the lower 48 were Florida and the new Cumberland Gap National Historical Park, located in adjoining parts of Kentucky, Tennessee and Virginia.

Where Do You Think You Are?

East or west, north or south, each of the distinctive areas above appeared on the road map of a single state in 1959. There is, as the saying goes, "no place like it." Can you identify the states?

Answers: 1-Ohio; 2-Maryland; 3-North Dakota; 4-Florida; 5-Nevada; 6-Alabama; 7-Kentucky; 8-Iowa; 9-Minnesota; 10-Colorado; 11-Utah; 12-Rhode Island

"Bon voyage!" cried the excited crowd in Manhattan as they waved goodbye to their friends bound for Europe by ship. How thrilling to have the opportunity to visit locations once only dreamed of.

This woman is determined to not miss an opportunity to photograph the sights in France. The artist is taken aback as she excitedly pushes in to snap the very scene he is painting.

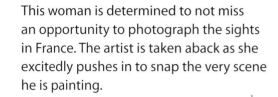

Away they go, bound for a location where there's plenty of green land and a wide-open sky. This family began the day full of energy and anticipation. By evening, everyone is worn out except for Mom and the family dog.

"Let me know if he bothers you."

Vacation Adventures

Water fun

This fisherman is having incredible luck. Each time he lands a big catch, the crowd shifts to the other side of the bridge. The fish seem to move where there are fewer people, or else this angler has discovered the perfect bait.

What fun it is to ski on an open lake. Dad is teaching his young daughter the fundamentals, and she is enjoying the ride.

The day at the beach has been so relaxing. Well, until it's time to find the car. No one remembers exactly where it is, which starts a family debate.

Hauling in fish is exciting, but the true joy of angling is enjoying the colors of a sunset and the peace of a quiet lake.

In the 1950s, ice-yacht clubs sprang up wherever there wasn't too much snow, but plenty of smooth ice.

Whether enjoyed for a day or a week, people love the beach. This is Dauphin Island, a narrow strip of sand 14 miles long near Alabama. It was a popular tourist attraction in the 1950s after a bridge linked the once remote island to the mainland.

Twice a year, kids were treated to a special alligator show at Riverside Park Zoo in Kansas. In the fall, when cooler weather made life uncomfortable for the warmth-loving reptiles, they were lifted by rope and pulley, and relocated to the basement of a building. In the spring, the process was reversed.

This fellow likes to roam the countryside and was photographed along U.S. Highway 36 in Missouri. He was an artist who had journeyed from Atlantic to Pacific and from Canada to Mexico at a speed of 10–12 miles a day.

With less than five feet separating their wingtips, the Navy flight demonstration squadron called the Blue Angels soar over Niagara Falls.

What appear to be rice patties are actually house lots in a suburb of Los Angeles with a spectacular view of the Pacific Ocean, Beverly Hills and Sunset Boulevard. Carved by bulldozer from the Santa Monica Mountains, the quarter-acre lots sold for $20,000–$75,000.

The Face of America

The Saturday Evening Post ran a series of articles called "The Face of America" in the magazine. The photographs showcased the immense diversity found in America, ranging from alligator relocation to ice harvesting, the photos captured Americans at their best in 1959.

In one of the few operations left in the nation, a crew harvests ice from Lake Sunapee in New Hampshire. Before modern refrigeration, ice was cut all winter.

These parents-to-be from Sacramento, Calif., are being taught how to care for a baby through a free American Red Cross class. The men seem to be enjoying the class as much as the women.

The Face of America

The Ladies' Aid group of St. Paul's Lutheran Church in Glasco, Kan., gathers to hand-quilt a bed coverlet. The quilt top features the Sunbonnet Sue design, "Parasol Lady." The ladies have snacks and chat with the pastor. The organist entertains by playing hymns. The art of quilting for these women has not changed much since the 1700s, though the event once included the whole countryside and ended with a party.

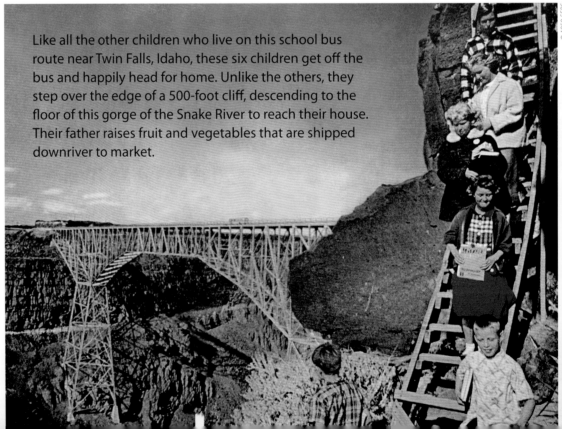

Like all the other children who live on this school bus route near Twin Falls, Idaho, these six children get off the bus and happily head for home. Unlike the others, they step over the edge of a 500-foot cliff, descending to the floor of this gorge of the Snake River to reach their house. Their father raises fruit and vegetables that are shipped downriver to market.

These sturdy and muscular men welding axes were part of the fun and games at the first annual Western Basque Festival at Sparks, Nev. The winner was awarded a prize of $50 for his efforts. He chopped through a 23-inch log in 3.25 minutes to win the event.

In Glen Falls, N.Y., these young brick layers take part in a contest for apprentices. The winner was awarded $200 in prize money and went on to the national championship in San Francisco. The competition that began in 1948 was intended to promote pride of craftsmanship among the students.

At St. Francis College in Fort Wayne, Ind., the old custom of a "school raising" was revived to meet the college's need for a science hall. Volunteers from nearby Indiana Technical College, along with students from St. Francis, supplied the labor. It took just eight hours to raise the building.

Choice Pastimes

It's Friday, and we have put in a long, hard week at work. When we arrive home, we are surprised by an offer from a friend to take part in a hobby and an amazing transformation takes place. The sparkle returns to our eyes and the spring to our step. How hobbies revive us!

Our attitude about the weather depends on our perspective. One man hoped for sunny skies so he could golf, while the gardener rejoices in every raindrop that falls.

"I'll see your August Social Security and raise you my September and October railroad pension."

This fellow gives up his favorite hobby to go antiquing with his wife. What is his reward? It's a broken chair that he'll be buying.

These women took up archery and entered competitions. The bows and arrows of 1959 were made of aluminum, laminated wood and plastic.

Young and old alike enjoyed playing bingo at the local volunteer fire department. To many, bingo meant a night out, alone or with friends. The profits provided funds for churches or other charitable organizations.

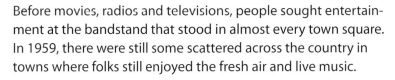

Before movies, radios and televisions, people sought entertainment at the bandstand that stood in almost every town square. In 1959, there were still some scattered across the country in towns where folks still enjoyed the fresh air and live music.

As the song says, "Take me out to the ballgame; take me out with the crowd. Buy me some peanuts and Cracker Jack. I don't care if I never get back!"

Do you remember some of Dr. Seuss' early books including *Yertle the Turtle*, *If I Ran the Zoo*, *Horton Hears a Who!* or *McElligot's Pool*? Fairy tales, Mother Goose rhymes and facts about dinosaurs or spaceships rounded out a child's book collection.

"We're slipping. Three o'clock on a rainy Saturday, and we still haven't driven them crazy."

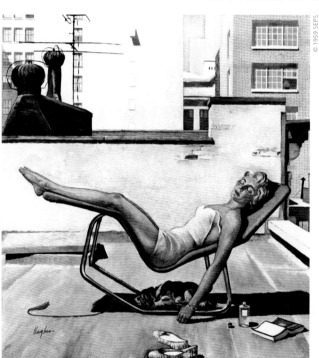

What could be more relaxing than the warmth of the sun, some time alone and a good book? It's so tranquil, in fact, the woman and her dog end up napping.

Choice Pastimes

Between the pages

Reading is more than a great way to acquire information. It is also a first-class pleasure as we delve into subjects and stories that fascinate us. Sometimes it's refreshing to slip away for time alone to enjoy a favorite story. At other times, reading books to children can strengthen family bonds.

Book sales were high in 1959 and offered a wealth of subjects to tempt young readers. Whatever the age or interests, a child could find fascinating experiences through the pages of a book.

Parents were advised to make sure their youngsters visited the local library early in life and often.

A nightly story time for children has two benefits. It shapes young minds and is also a relaxing activity before bedtime.

Best-Selling Books of 1959

Exodus
by Leon Uris

Doctor Zhivago
by Boris Pasternak

Hawaii
by James A. Michener

Advise and Consent
by Allen Drury

Lady Chatterley's Lover
by D.H. Lawrence

The Ugly American
by Eugene L. Burdick and William Lederer

Dear and Glorious Physician
by Taylor Caldwell

Lolita
by Vladmir Nabokov

Mrs. 'Arris Goes to Paris
by Paul Gallico

Poor No More
by Robert Ruark

Cover Artist, Constantin Alajalov

Constantin Alajalov was a Russian native, born in Rostov in 1900. He was a student at the University of Petrograd during the October Revolution. He survived this difficult time by joining a government-organized group of artists who traveled the country to paint large propaganda posters and murals. At age 23, he had earned enough money to purchase his passage to the United States. He sold his first cover to *The New Yorker*, progressing to *The Saturday Evening Post* for the October 6, 1945 edition. Alajalov used a style of line drawing that was similar to a cartoon or caricature, but with added detail, color and storytelling.

The illustrations on this spread are Alajalov's *Saturday Evening Post* covers of 1959. By age 62 he had painted a total of 73 covers for *The Post*. He continued with his artwork for many years, dying at age 87.

What Made Us Laugh

"Some good came of it—you've stopped smoking."

"George—he isn't ours!"

"He's our bouncer."

"I've got him talking to himself."

"It's very realistic, complete with plumbing that goes haywire, appliances that don't work and backbreaking payments."

"Of course, I'd be more impressed with Dickie's proposal if he hadn't sent the telegram 'collect.'"

"You're working too hard, Ralph."

"Hi, Freddie, and everybody on the extensions …."

The center of attraction in this room was the bathtub that could be accessed from three sides. All of the American Standard fixtures came in white and many popular colors.

Teens enjoyed their own rooms and often requested the use of bright, bold colors and eye-catching wallpaper.

Extra living space was found in this home by enclosing the back porch and converting the area into a fun family room.

Built-in appliances were one of the most modern kitchen looks for 1959. Color dominated the interior design of homes, carrying through to appliances as well.

1959 Decor

The bare wood floors that were in most older homes were disappearing. Instead, vinyl floor coverings were installed. The vinyl was easier to clean than the wood floors that often had cracks between the boards where dust and dirt could hide. The layer of foam underneath the vinyl was also easier on the feet.

The kitchen above had an oriental flavor with Armstrong custom vinyl floor inlays. At left, families made use of all possible living space. This area was at one time an attic, but it was converted into a comfortable family hideaway, complete with fireplace. The furniture in both rooms reflected the clean, contemporary look of what was sold during the era.

HOOVER

The new Hoover electric floor washer, above, cleaned floors and suctioned up the scrub water. Hands never touched the dirt! The canister vacuum cleaner at right was the first with an on-off switch on the handle.

Give her a HOOVER. and you give her the best!

Home Conveniences

Manufacturers continued to introduce home conveniences that caused housewives to wonder what they ever did without them. Prior to Tupperware®, foods were stored in glass, metal or crockery dishes. Women were taught how to "burp" the Tupperware bowls, a catchy phrase for the method used to seal the plastic containers.

Home-based Tupperware parties were fun and proved to be a successful way to sell large amounts of the versatile and convenient plastic products.

FAMOUS BIRTHDAYS
Allison Janney, November 19 actress (C.J. Cregg of *The West Wing*)
Judd Nelson, November 28 actor (*The Breakfast Club*)

Westinghouse 1000

This washing machine had more cycle selections and an automatic lint ejector that sent scum down the drain.

FRIGIDAIRE

The woman with the stylish refrigerator above felt like a queen. Best of all, it was frost-free.

Young homeowners could meet their family's sewing needs with a Singer sewing machine.

GENERAL ⓖⓔ ELECTRIC

The dishes were done in the time it took to clear the table and put them in the dishwasher. No more "dishpan" hands!

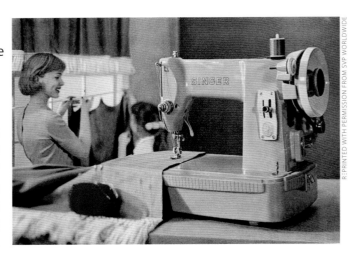

The real good meat from the sea

This is Star-Kist—the prime tuna that's good enough to serve like meat. Stands to reason it tastes meatier and heartier, no matter how you use it. In casseroles, salads, sandwiches, or any other way you enjoy tuna.

Star-Kist® tuna continues to be a handy convenience food that is still used in casseroles and sandwiches.

Star-Kist
CHUNK LIGHT TUNA

"RC?
I *prefer* it"

Royal Crown COLA

Meet the cola with the *fresh* up-to-date difference—today's RC. Distinctive—with a bright, sprightly, delightfully less sweet taste all its own (made from fresh, protected concentrate instead of perishable syrup). Try ice-cold RC and see. D-e-l-i-c-i-o-u-s!

You'll prefer  **Royal Crown COLA** the *fresher* refresher

The top crop's in!

Milky sweet and begging for **Land O'Lakes** Sweet Cream **Butter***

A full ½ gallon of country-fresh sweet cream in every pound

⊕LIGHTLY SALTED OR UNSALTED

Land O'Lakes butter has been sold since the 1920s and set the standard for butter quality.

From the Grocery Store

Home conveniences also expanded to the grocery store. In 1959, grocery shelves were stocked with an abundance of processed and ready-to-eat foods. There were canned and frozen foods that were quick and easy to prepare, giving busy housewives more time for activities outside the kitchen.

M-m-m-m ...that chicken*

*fried with **MRS TUCKER'S** SHORTENING

1959 ANDERSON, CLAYTON & CO.

Mrs. Tucker's shortening was used to make delicious, crispy fried chicken.

Chun King dinners were the easy way to enjoy Chinese food. The frozen product included egg rolls and rice in every meal.

If you know your oats, you'll go for

Cheerios'
all 'round
toasted crispness

Cheerios

THE OAT CEREAL REAL

Cheerios, originally named CheeriOats, was one of the top-selling cold cereals for General Mills. The taste and wholesome appeal of oats, a hot breakfast staple for decades, was the main selling point.

Happy eating... quick and easy!

Chicken! Shrimp! Beef! Try all three...

Cantonese style Dinner

CHUN KING

REPRINTED WITH PERMISSION FROM CONAGRA FOODS, OMAHA, NEBRASKA

From the Grocery Store

1959 recipes

New idea from *Betty Crocker*

"Lot o' Little Cakes"

from Betty Crocker White Cake Mix!

LOT O' LITTLE CAKES

HERE'S YOUR VERY SECRET SECRET— Use Betty Crocker White Cake Mix (or any of our layer cake mixes). Each package makes about 50 little cakes.

How to bake	**How to frost**	**How to cut**	**How to trim**
Heat oven to 350°. Make batter as directed. Spread in greased and floured jelly roll pan, 15½ x10½ x1". Bake about 25 minutes. Cool in pan. Frost and cut your cake as shown in the diagrams at right. Then let your imagination take over for the prettiest teacakes in town!	Make up Betty Crocker Fluffy White Frosting Mix. Divide into small bowls; tint. Frost cake sections with different colors.	Diamonds Squares Triangles	A variety of pretty decorations give your little cakes a personal touch. Use • make your own or buy ready-made rosettes • chopped nuts • silver shot • gumdrops • candy sprinkles • chocolate bits • maraschino cherries

...and of course you know

"We guarantee a perfect* cake—homemade-perfect

cake...after cake...after cake!"

Betty Crocker General Mills

Wonderful bread even a bride can bake— our Anadama Batter Bread!

¾ cup boiling water	¼ cup warm water
½ cup yellow	(not hot—110° to 115°)
corn meal	1 pkg. active dry yeast
3 tbsp. shortening	1 egg
¼ cup molasses	2¾ cups sifted Gold Medal
2 tsp. salt	"Kitchen Tested" Flour

Stir first 5 ingredients in large mixer bowl. Cool to lukewarm. Dissolve yeast in warm water. Add yeast, egg, half of flour to mixture. Beat 2 min. med. speed, scraping bowl frequently. Add rest of flour; mix with spoon until well blended. Spread evenly in greased loaf pan, 8½ x4½ x2¾". Batter will be sticky. Flour hands, smooth top of loaf. Set in warm place (85°) until batter reaches top of pan, about 1½ hr. (If kitchen is cool, place on rack over a bowl of hot water and cover with towel.) Sprinkle top with corn meal and salt. Bake 50 to 55 min. at 375°. Crust will be dark brown. Remove from pan immediately and set on rack to cool.

Betty Crocker continues to be a trusted name brand. Recipes are often included on the product packaging and in ads to promote the use of the products.

The Metro Daily News FINAL EDITION

DECEMBER 5, 1959

OPERATION PETTICOAT MOVIE IS RELEASED

This World War II–era comedy stars Cary Grant, Tony Curtis and Joan O'Brien.

for breakfast: *Sticky Buns . . . with Brer Rabbit Molasses, Brown 'n Serve Rolls*

BRER RABBIT STICKY BUN RECIPE

In each section of muffin pan put ¼ teaspoon butter or margarine, 1 tablespoon Brer Rabbit Molasses (Green Label) and a sprinkling of nuts. Place Brown 'n Serve Rolls upside down in each section. Bake at 400°F. for 9 minutes. Remove immediately from pan and drizzle buns with molasses mixture.

BETTY CROCKER PINEAPPLE-CARAMEL-NUT ROLL RECIPE

¼ cup Brer Rabbit Molasses (Gold Label)
¼ cup granulated sugar
¼ cup butter
9-oz. can crushed pineapple
½ cup pecan halves
12 Brown 'n Serve Rolls

Heat oven to 375° (quick mod.). Stir molasses, sugar and butter in small pan over medium heat until butter is melted and a smooth syrup forms. Put about 1 tbsp. syrup in each of 12 medium muffin cups. Sprinkle 3 or 4 pecan halves over syrup. Drain pineapple; divide equally between muffin cups. Place unbaked Brown 'n Serve Rolls, right-side-up, on top of mixture; bake 15 min. Invert immediately. Let stand a few minutes before removing. Serve pineapple-side-up.

for lunch or supper: *Hot Tuna Salad Ring . . . Breast O' Chicken Tuna, Brown 'n Serve Rolls*

HOT TUNA SALAD RING

6½-oz. can Breast O' Chicken Tuna, chunk or solid pack
1 cup thinly sliced celery
1 cup toasted Brown 'n Serve cubes
¼ cup chopped toasted almonds
¼ tsp. salt
1 tsp. grated onion
½ cup mayonnaise
1 tbsp. lemon juice
¼ cup grated cheese

Heat oven to 425° (hot). Combine all ingredients—except ½ cup toasted cubes and cheese. Pile lightly in 1-qt. baking dish. Sprinkle with cheese and cubes. Bake 10 to 12 min. 4 servings.

Separate 1 pkg. Brown 'n Serve Cloverleaf Rolls. Brush sides with beaten egg white. Arrange close together in buttered 10" ring mold, rounded-side-up. Bake 10 to 12 min. at 425° (hot). Remove from oven and brush tops with melted butter. Turn out onto serving plate rounded-side-up, and fill center with Hot Tuna Salad. Garnish with pimiento, slices of lemon, twisted, and sprigs of parsley around edge of plate.

General Mills introduced a new brown-and-serve process to America's cooks in 1949. For the first time, homemakers could serve their families hot rolls that were premade, but browned in their own ovens. To celebrate the 10th anniversary of the product, the company created a booklet of easy, tasty recipe ideas like those shown above.

Every weekday... Sunday, too!
Campbell's Soups are <u>good</u> for you!

Enjoy *Campbell's* VEGETABLE SOUP

15 GARDEN VEGETABLES AND STURDY BEEF STOCK ... here's a soup your whole family enjoys—Campbell's Vegetable Soup. Every delicious bowlful is filled with the goodness of 15 green and yellow vegetables picked at their flavor peak. M'm! Good! *Nourishing* good! Ready in 4 minutes... less than 7¢ a serving! So easy to enjoy the happy habit...

ONCE A DAY...<u>EVERY</u> DAY...SOUP!

Have <u>you</u> had your soup today?

Campbell's CONDENSED VEGETABLE SOUP MADE WITH BEEF STOCK

Campbell's Vegetable Soup gives you Vitamins, Proteins... Minerals, too!

REPRINTED WITH PERMISSION FROM CAMPBELL SOUP CO.

Adorable Mascots

Of all the advertising mascots seen in the 1950s, two of the most adorable were the Campbell's Soup Kids and Northern's American Beauties. Grace Drayton, an illustrator and writer, was the creator of the Campbell's Soup Kids that helped to sell Campbell's Soup since 1904. The company's advertising agents loved their appeal and chose them as the official trademarks.

In the late 1950s, Northern began using a new marketing and packaging approach for their tissue. Frances Hook's illustrations of sweet little girls were selected as a symbol for softness. The "American Beauties," as they were called, proved to be popular and effectively increased Northern's sales.

Boy, oh, boy! Beef Noodle!

REPRINTED WITH PERMISSION FROM CAMPBELL SOUP CO.

REPRINTED WITH PERMISSION FROM CAMPBELL SOUP CO.

REPRINTED WITH PERMISSION FROM CAMPBELL SOUP CO.

NEW—
AND LOVELY
FOR YOU

*"Pretty girl" packages
don't they say
Softness is Northern
in a wonderful way?*

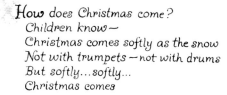

*How does Christmas come?
Children know—
Christmas comes softly as the snow
Not with trumpets—not with drums
But softly...softly...
Christmas comes*

*Soft as the sound of a tiny hoof
Tippy-toe tapping
Up on the roof!*

*Soft as the tiptoe sounds downstairs
(They think we're asleep
Having heard our prayers)*

*Soft as the rustle of wondrous wings
Soft as the anthem
A far choir sings*

*Soft as the wonder of years gone by
When a Mother crooned a lullabye...
While a star stood high
In the Christmas sky.*

The delightful Northern "American Beauties" were so popular that art prints were also produced and sold.

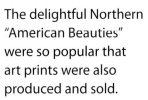

*All of us—the grownups who make
Northern Tissue—join our
little girls in wishing you
a truly joyous Christmas*

Christmas Cheer

Christmas could be a trying holiday for husbands. When the poor man at left was done wrestling with his wife's present, everyone would know that only Dad could have made a gift look that wrinkled and rumpled. But it was no doubt wrapped with love. So was the gift below, but in this case, the wife was less than thrilled with the contents. Take this advice, men: You don't have to spend a lot of money, according to these illustrations, to make your wife happy. Just don't give her a housekeeping item!

More *The Saturday Evening Post* Covers

The Saturday Evening Post covers were works of art, many illustrated by famous artists of the time, including Norman Rockwell. Most of the 1959 covers have been incorporated within the previous pages of this book; the few that were not are presented on the following pages for your enjoyment.

The Saturday Evening
POST
March 14, 1959 – 15¢

THE MOST FATEFUL
TWENTY-FOUR HOURS
OF OUR TIME:

D DAY

As Recounted by
The Men Who Lived Through It

The Saturday Evening
POST
March 28, 1959 – 15¢

Pete Martin calls on
MARY MARTIN

WHICH DEMOCRAT IN '60?
By STEWART ALSOP

The Saturday Evening
POST
May 23, 1959 – 15¢

The Untold Story
of Little Rock

By VIRGIL T. BLOSSOM
Superintendent of Little Rock Schools, 1953–1958

The Saturday Evening
POST
July 4, 1959 – 15¢

HOW HOFFA
GOT THAT WAY
By JOHN BARTLOW MARTIN

WALTER REED HOSPITAL
By BEVERLY SMITH, JR.

The Saturday Evening POST

July 25, 1959 – 15¢

The Rockefeller Nobody Knows
By STEWART ALSOP

Tony Curtis's Winning Battle
By ROBERT JOHNSON

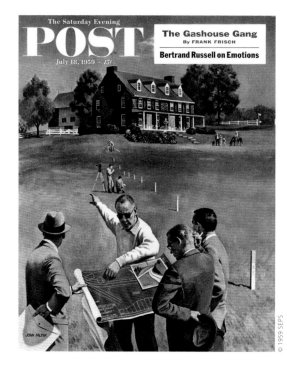

The Saturday Evening POST

July 18, 1959 – 15¢

The Gashouse Gang
By FRANK FRISCH

Bertrand Russell on Emotions

JOHN FALTER

The Saturday Evening POST

August 29, 1959 – 15¢

ARE WE ENDANGERING THE LIVES OF OUR CHILDREN'S CHILDREN?

A Complete Report on

Fallout: The Silent Killer

The Saturday Evening POST

October 10, 1959 – 15¢

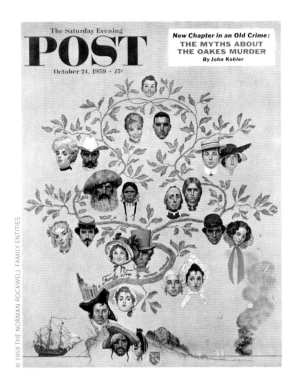

The Saturday Evening
POST
October 24, 1959 – 15¢

New Chapter in an Old Crime:
**THE MYTHS ABOUT
THE OAKES MURDER**
By John Kobler

The Saturday Evening
POST
November 14, 1959 – 20¢

Hollywood Lawyer
JERRY GIESLER
Tells His Own Story

The Saturday Evening
POST
November 21, 1959 – 15¢

JERRY GIESLER'S Own Story:
The CHARLIE CHAPLIN Case

A Short Story by JOHN O'HARA

MODERN BUILDERS CORP.

SIDEWALK SUPERINTENDENTS

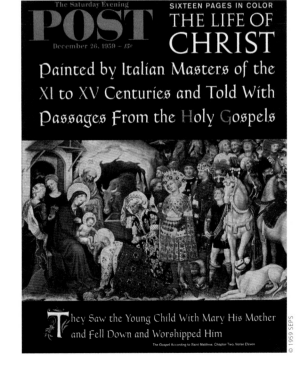

The Saturday Evening
POST
December 26, 1959 – 15¢

SIXTEEN PAGES IN COLOR
**THE LIFE OF
CHRIST**

Painted by Italian Masters of the
XI to XV Centuries and Told With
Passages From the Holy Gospels

They Saw the Young Child With Mary His Mother
and Fell Down and Worshipped Him

The Gospel According to Saint Matthew, Chapter Two, Verse Eleven

MORE FAMOUS BIRTHDAYS

January 7
Kathy Valentine, bassist (The Go-Go's)

January 9
Otis Nixon, Jr., baseball outfielder (Atlanta Braves, Cleveland Indians)

January 15
Kenny Easley, NFL safety (Seattle Seahawks)

January 17
Susanna Hoffs, musician, lead singer (The Bangles)

January 27
Chris Collinsworth, TV sportscaster, NFL wide receiver (Cincinnati Bengals)

January 28
Frank Darabont, film director (*The Shawshank Redemption*)

January 30
Mark Eitzel, musician (American Music Club)

February 2
Dexter Manley, NFL defensive end (Washington Redskins)

February 4
Pamelyn Ferdin, actress, animal rights protestor

February 10
John Calipari, head basketball coach (University of Kentucky)

February 14
Renée Fleming, opera singer (recent album *Poémes*, 2012)

February 15
Ali Campbell, lead singer (UB40)
Joseph R. Gannascoli, actor (Vito of *The Sopranos*)

February 20
Bill Gullickson, baseball pitcher (Montreal Expos, Detroit Tigers)

February 24
Beth Broderick, actress (Aunt Zelda of *Sabrina, the Teenage Witch*)

March 7
Tom Lehman, PGA golfer
Mike Nolan, football coach (San Francisco 49ers)

March 8
Aidan Quinn, actor (Lt. Kevin Sweeney of *Prime Suspect*)
Lester Holt, NBC reporter, weekend anchor (*NBC Nightly News*)

March 14
Tamara Tunie, actress (Alberta Green of *24*)

March 16
Michael J Bloomfield, NASA astronaut

March 18
Irene Cara, actress, singer

March 20
Sting (AKA Steve Borden), professional wrestler

March 22
Matthew Modine, actor (Joker of *Full Metal Jacket*)

April 2
David Frankel, film director (*The Devil Wears Prada*)

April 10
Brian Setzer, musician (Stray Cats)

April 17
Sean Bean, actor (Boromir of *Lord of the Rings*)

April 20
Clint Howard, actor (Mark Wedloe of *Gentle Ben*)

April 22
Ryan Stiles, actor (*Whose Line Is It Anyway?*)

April 24
Glenn Morshower, actor (Aaron Pierce of *24*)

April 27
Nicholas D. Kristof, journalist (*New York Times*)
Sheena Easton, actress, singer ("My Baby Takes the Morning Train")

April 30
Paul Gross, actor (*Due South*)

May 1
Eddie Johnson, NBA forward (Kansas City/ Sacramento Kings, Houston Rockets, Indiana Pacers)

May 3
Ben Elton, comic, screenwriter (*Blackadder*)

May 4
Bob Tway, PGA golfer (1986 PGA Championship)

May 8
Ronnie Lott, NFL safety (San Francisco 49ers, Los Angeles Raiders)

May 11
Martha Quinn, TV personality (original MTV veejay)

May 16
Andrew Litton, conductor (Bergen Philharmonic)

May 20
Bronson Pinchot, actor (Balki of *Perfect Strangers*)

May 26
Kevin Gage, actor (*Heat*)

May 29
Adrian Paul, actor (*Highlander*)
Rupert Everett, actor (*My Best Friend's Wedding*)

June 3
Sam Mills, NFL linebacker (New Orleans Saints, Carolina Panthers)

June 6
Amanda Pays, actress (Theora Jones of *Max Headroom*)
James Samuel "Jimmy Jam" Harris III, songwriter, musician, producer

June 11
Hugh Laurie, actor (Dr. Gregory House of *House*)

June 15
Eileen Davidson, actress (Ashley Abbott of *The Bold and the Beautiful*)

June 21
Tom Chambers, NBA forward/center (Seattle SuperSonics, Phoenix Suns)

July 1
Dale Midkiff, actor (*Love Comes Softly*)

July 5
Marc Cohn, singer/songwriter ("Walking in Memphis")

July 7
Billy Campbell, actor (*The Rocketeer*)

July 9
Jim Kerr, singer (Simple Minds)
Kevin Nash, professional wrestler, actor

July 11
Richie Sambora, guitarist (Bon Jovi)
Suzanne Vega, musician ("Luka")

July 13
Joe Lockhart, White House press secretary under President Clinton

August 2
Victoria Jackson, comic (*Saturday Night Live*)

August 13
Danny Bonaduce, actor (Danny of *The Partridge Family*)

August 14
Marcia Gay Harden, actress (Verna of *Miller's Crossing*)

August 21
Jim McMahon, NFL quarterback (Chicago Bears)

August 22
Collin Raye, country musician ("I Think About You")

August 24
Linda Hogan, TV personality (ex-wife of Hulk Hogan)

August 29
Rebecca De Mornay, actress (*And God Created Woman*)
Stephen Wolfram, mathematician, computer programmer (creator of *Mathematica*)

September 11
John Hawkes, actor (Bugsy of *The Perfect Storm*)

September 14
Mary Crosby, daughter of Bing and Kathryn Crosby, actress (Kristin Shepard of *Dallas*)

September 21
Chris Goss, heavy rock producer and musician

September 22
Wally Backman, second baseman (New York Mets, Seattle Mariners)

September 23
Jason Alexander, actor (George Costanza of *Seinfeld*)

September 28
Todd Worrell, pitcher (St. Louis Cardinals, Los Angeles Dodgers)

October 3
Fred Couples, PGA golfer (1992 Masters Tournament winner)
Jack Wagner, actor (Frisco Jones of *General Hospital*)

October 10
Bradley Whitford, actor (Josh Lyman of *The West Wing*)
Julia Sweeney, comic (Androgyne Pat of *Saturday Night Live*)

October 15
Sarah Ferguson, Duchess of York (ex-wife of Prince Andrew)

October 21
George Bell, left fielder (Toronto Blue Jays, Chicago White Sox)
Ken Watanabe, actor (*The Last Samurai*)

October 23
Sam Raimi, film director (*Spider-Man* movies)

October 31
Michael DeLorenzo, actor (*A Few Good Men*)

November 2
Peter Mullan, actor (*My Name Is Joe*)

November 7
Billy Gillispie, college basketball coach (Texas Tech)

November 9
Donnie McClurkin, gospel singer

November 10
Mackenzie Phillips, actress (Julie of *One Day at a Time*)

November 16
Corey Allen Pavin, PGA golfer

November 26
Jamie Rose, actress (Vickie Gioberti of *Falcon Crest*)

November 29
Rich Camarillo, NFL punter (New England Patriots, Houston Oilers)

December 10
Mark Aguirre, NBA forward (Dallas Mavericks, Detroit Pistons)

December 13
Jim Harrell, professional wrestler
Johnny Whitaker, actor (Jody of *Family Affair*)

December 15
Heidi Bohay, actress (Megan Kendall of *Hotel*)

December 28
Everson Walls, NFL cornerback (Dallas Cowboys, New York Giants)

December 29
Patricia Clarkson, actress (*Pieces of April*)

December 30
Tracey Ullman, comic (*The Tracey Ullman Show*)

Facts and Figures of 1959

President of the U.S.
Dwight D. Eisenhower
Vice President of the U.S.
Richard M. Nixon

Population of the U.S.
177,830,000

Births
4,245,000

High School Graduates
Males: 784,000
Females: 843,000

Average salary for full-time employee: $5,061
Minimum wage (per hour): $1.00
Unemployment rate: 5.5%
Rate of inflation: 1.01%

COURTESY NATIONAL PARK SERVICE, EISENHOWER NATIONAL HISTORIC SITE, ENHS 1031

© 1959 SEPS

Average cost for:

Bread (lb.) $0.20

Bacon (lb.) $0.67

Butter (lb.) $0.75

Eggs (doz.) $0.53

Milk (½ gal.) $0.51

Potatoes (10 lbs.) $0.63

Coffee (lb.) $0.78

Sugar (5 lbs.) $0.57

Gasoline (gal.) $0.25

Movie ticket $0.51

Postage stamp $0.04

New home $12,400

© GETTY IMAGES

Notable Inventions and Firsts

January 25: With the Boeing 707, American Airlines begins the first regularly scheduled jet service between New York and Los Angeles.

Spring: A new fad spreads across college campuses, as students stuff themselves into phone booths.

August 7: The U.S. Navy announces that it has developed a radar system that can monitor, from U.S. bases, Soviet nuclear tests and missile launches.

September 11: Congress passes a bill that will provide food stamps for low-income Americans.

October 2: CBS introduces Rod Serling's *The Twilight Zone*, a sci-fi television series with strong social commentary.

October 23: Juanita Kidd Stout is appointed Judge of the Common Pleas Court in Philadelphia, becoming the first black female judge in the United States.

November 24: The United States and the Soviet Union sign a pact in which they agree to collaborate on advancements in science, sports and culture.

December 14: Berry Gordy founds Motown Records in Detroit.

1959: The U.S. mint begins to print the Lincoln Memorial on the penny in honor of the 16th president's 150th birthday.

1959: Häagen-Dazs ice cream and Hawaiian Punch fruit drink are the latest additions to American supermarket shelves.

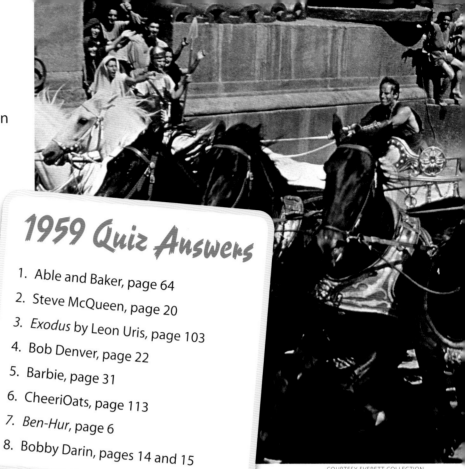

COURTESY EVERETT COLLECTION

1959 Quiz Answers

1. Able and Baker, page 64
2. Steve McQueen, page 20
3. *Exodus* by Leon Uris, page 103
4. Bob Denver, page 22
5. Barbie, page 31
6. CheeriOats, page 113
7. *Ben-Hur*, page 6
8. Bobby Darin, pages 14 and 15

NATIONAL BASEBALL HALL OF FAME LIBRARY COOPERSTOWN, N.Y.

Sports Winners

NFL: Baltimore Colts defeat New York Giants
World Series: Los Angeles Dodgers defeat Chicago White Sox
Stanley Cup: Montreal Canadiens defeat Toronto Maple Leafs
The Masters: Art Wall
PGA Championship: Bob Rosburg
NBA: Boston Celtics defeat Minneapolis Lakers

Live It Again 1959

PROJECT EDITOR	Barb Sprunger
CREATIVE DIRECTOR	Brad Snow
COPYWRITER & RESEARCH ASSISTANT	Becky Sarasin
EDITORIAL ASSISTANT	Laurie Lehman
COPY SUPERVISOR	Deborah Morgan
PRODUCTION ARTIST SUPERVISOR	Erin Brandt
PRODUCTION ARTIST	Edith Teegarden
COPY EDITORS	Mary O'Donnell, Sam Schneider
PHOTOGRAPHY SUPERVISOR	Tammy Christian
NOSTALGIA EDITOR	Ken Tate
PUBLISHING SERVICES DIRECTOR	Brenda Gallmeyer

Printed in China
First Printing: 2012
Library of Congress Control Number: 2012939373

Customer Service
LiveItAgain.com
(800) 829-5865

1 2 3 4 5 6 7 8 9